PRAISE for *Take Your Mark, LEAD!*

"*Take Your Mark, LEAD! is a book that both athletic and corporate teams can utilize to raise their performance. Its discussion guide in the back of the book is valuable for creating conversations and providing potential for individual and team growth. If you want to up your game, this is a leadership and performance book to explore.*"

—**Teri McKeever,** US Olympic and Cal Berkeley Head Swim Coach

"*Some leadership books can be boring, but this book will entertain you with stories and examples of great strategies to make you better in your personal life and as a leader. I never thought a self-help book could be a page-turner, but this one is!*"

—**Rosario Londono**, Social Innovator, Adjunct Professor, American University

"*Kelly knows the roadmap, the granular details to achieving the Champion inside you. She brings real-world experience to her conclusions on leadership and performance.*"

—**Mel Stewart,** Olympic Champion, Co-Founder of SwimSwam

"*Kelly is an incandescent light that cuts through the fog limiting your potential. Get ready for your life and leadership skills to level up!*"

—**Peter T. Yu,** MD, MPH, FACS, FAAP, Pediatric general & thoracic surgeon

"*Take Your Mark, LEAD! is motivational, organized, and inspiring. It has something for everyone. It is food for thought, with invaluable insights to help bring out the inner champion and leader in every reader.*"

—**Markos Papadatos**, Editor-at-Large, Digital Journal

More PRAISE

"Kelly, I peeked at your book during a quick break and an hour later I'm still reading! Captivating stories, well told and brilliantly summarized with practical calls to action! The book has a brilliant presentation of bite-size, digestible and actionable things ANYONE can do immediately to be, to love, serve and lead better!"

—**Tina Andrew**, General Manager, NY Breakers

"Kelly Parker Palace defines leadership. Whether guiding and encouraging others or getting prominent athletes to discuss leadership in their lives, Kelly generates a spark within individuals that prompts them to believe anything is attainable."

—**John Lohn**, Associate Editor-in-Chief, Swimming World News

"Five enthusiastic, self-help stars. Take Your Mark, LEAD! is a book that I will keep by my bedside, dog-ear the pages, and write in the margins for continual growth. You don't have to be CEO to find worth in the lines on these pages. I've already implemented this book into my everyday life and am reaping the benefits."

—**Stephie Walls,** Best-Selling Author, stephiewalls.com

"Understanding the mindset of a champion is the most valuable asset an athlete or a coach can possess. Having the ability to learn from masters of our craft is a joyful luxury. This book is exactly that. Kelly's real life experiences prove dreams come true."

—**Cody Miller,** Olympic Champion, YouTube Celebrity

TAKE YOUR MARK,

LEAD!

TAKE YOUR MARK, LEAD!

10 Ways to Lead Yourself and Others

LIKE A CHAMPION

Cover design and writing coaching by Genevieve Parker Hill
GenevieveParkerHill.com

Editing and collaboration by Nancy Laforest
nancylaforestpro@gmail.com

Book design by Carlene Vitale

ISBN: 978-1-7371069-0-6

Library of Congress Cataloging-in-publication Data:

Names: Parker Palace, Kelly, author

Title: Take Your Mark, LEAD!—10 Ways to Lead Yourself and Others Like a Champion
First Edition

Description: Kelly Parker Palace, Florida, 2021

Identifiers: ISBN 978-1-7371069-0-6 (Perfect bound)
ASIN: B0937N15N7 (eBook)
ISBN: 9798200701926 (Audiobook)

Subjects: | Non-Fiction | Leadership | Personal Development | Self-help |
Printed in the United States of America on acid-free paper.

More products and services from Kelly Parker Palace at KellyPalace.com

Also available as an audiobook, by Blackstone Publishing, wherever audiobooks are found.

24   23   22   21   8   7   6   5   4   3   2   1

DEDICATION

To my late Mother and my Dad
for lovingly leading me towards the right path.

And to Genevieve, for leading me to finish this book.

CONTENTS

FOREWORD

by Bob Bowman

4X Olympic Coach
Coach of the greatest Olympian of all time, Michael Phelps
Head Coach, Arizona State University, Men's & Women's Swimming

The world of high-performance athletics is a pressure-filled incubator for life skills. To succeed, athletes must learn how to set goals, develop plans to achieve them, solve problems, build productive habits, and ultimately survive success upon reaching the next milestone. Coaches are the leaders of this process, doing our best each day to instill the values, habits, and work ethic which will ultimately give the best chance of success to those in our care. Effective leaders are keen observers of their teams. They are responsible for creating an environment where each member can thrive and grow. They understand the principles of human performance but most importantly, they understand people. They can offer support, guidance, and inspiration. They lead by example, walking the talk. Coaches build trust and earn respect by how they act and interact with their teams. They ignite the fire of discovery and cheer their teams to victory.

However, the path of a champion is not easy. It is filled with disappointment and failure. The great ones understand that setbacks are the prime opportunity to learn and grow. They are the stepping stones to higher levels of performance and the means by which leaders are made. As I often tell my swimmers, good judgment comes from experience. Experience comes from bad judgment and sometimes bad luck. We all make mistakes and must deal with obstacles in our efforts to accomplish our objectives in life. The key is how we learn from experiences we encounter along the way. Positive leadership is the catalyst for this process.

Kelly Parker Palace has lived both sides of this equation, having been a champion athlete and a groundbreaking coach. Also a champion of causes, she has learned the hard lessons and perfected the skills that lead to sustained success and lasting satisfaction. I have known Kelly as a coach and during wonderful conversations on her *Champion's Mojo* podcast. She is acutely interested in both the art and science behind top-level performance, whether in the pool, in business, or in personal life. Her love of this pursuit is brought to life in this book, illustrated by her own life experiences and those who are leading coaches, athletes, and competitors in other fields. Her personal testimony is powerful and I found it to be highly motivational.

Take Your Mark, LEAD! will explain the qualities of effective leaders and outline different types of leadership styles. It will show you how to use proven methods of psychology to set goals, visualize success and ultimately perform at the critical moment. Kelly will show you how to foster habits that will build a lifestyle where personal excellence is inevitable. She will share her personal story and the lessons learned in the journey of being an athlete, coach, and businesswoman.

Kelly has been thinking out of the box her entire life. As a decorated athlete, she excelled at the highest levels of her sport. In the male-dominated field of swim coaching, she was an accomplished Division One head coach with a clear vision and a strong voice. She has carried this passion to her business endeavors and continues to conquer challenges as she inspires countless others to be their best selves. As you read these chapters, you too will know her enthusiasm, energy, and wisdom. Each of these lessons is delivered in a way that anyone can benefit from and use in daily life. The action steps following each chapter will be powerful opportunities to build your personal leadership toolbox.

As Ralph Nader so succinctly said, "The function of leadership is to produce more leaders, not more followers." Every chapter of this book will bring this idea to life. You are about to embark on a voyage of self-discovery. You will learn how to improve performance in any endeavor you undertake, how to build a more purposeful and goal-directed life and, most importantly, how to help others do the same.

The best time to begin is always now. Therefore, in the language of the swimming world, I'm excited to say, *"Take your mark..."*

—Bob Bowman

PREFACE

It has taken me ten years to write this book. It was born out of the desire to help others benefit from the techniques and skills that I acquired as an athlete and coach, which transferred to success in the corporate and business world—beyond what I could have imagined. After leaving college coaching, I rocketed up the corporate ladder of a *Fortune* 100 company with seven promotions in ten years. A bit shocked by my rise, I wondered, *how did that happen*? In my first year in my corporate job, I doubled my annual income from being a coach, then the next year I doubled *that* annual income as well. That included getting what was purported to be one of the largest sales bonuses in the company's 100 year-plus history. *Now, how did that happen*?! It was not all about the money—although sometimes money can be a barometer of what you are giving to the world. I simply loved the challenge of taking the next rung. After a decade of leading in corporate America, I left to become an entrepreneur and, over the next several years, built a multi-million dollar business. Hmmm, *how the heck did that happen*?! In 2012, I co-founded a charity that helps millions of people around the globe and is challenging the fundamentals of the way a common medical condition is treated. *Whoa, how did that happen*?!

What I discovered was that, even though I have no special gifts or talents for the things I attained, I earned these results by applying the strategies I learned from my days as a competitive swimmer and coach. And I believe anyone can do the same. The coach in me wants to coach others to reach their full potential, and I thought a book would be the best way to share this message.

Continually, as I noted others around me hitting higher and higher levels, I kept asking, *how exactly did that happen*? I began to observe all the leaders and champions who ended up in this book and gleaned, or asked them directly, *how they had made their success happen.*

With journalism as my undergraduate major and a lifelong passion, over the next decade I chronicled these lessons. This book's original working title was *Take Your Mark, Make Your Mark, Using Athletic Techniques to Achieve Your Dreams*. Then upon closer examination of the actions and principles that were driving achievements, both mine and others', I observed that peak performance really comes down to leadership. I started scrutinizing everything from the lens of exemplary leadership and *how that happens*. That's when this book became *Take Your Mark, LEAD!*

Then life happened, as it always does, and I was sidelined for years with a debilitating illness, followed by caring for my mother with Alzheimer's, my own breast cancer, and then having to move out while renovating our oceanfront home, twice, after it was hit by two hurricanes—none of which are conducive to much writing. But I chipped away, working at it when I could, and building a file of the ideal characteristics that one needs to lead like a champion. The pandemic allowed me to write for the last year and finally cross the finish line.

Now that this book is written and I have reached another big milestone, I no longer have to ask *how it happened*. It's more clear than ever that these strategies can be utilized to lead yourself and others to grand accomplishments. I'm hopeful that this book will have the positive impact on your life that I envision it can. I am utterly grateful that you are here.

INTRODUCTION

How do certain people make a mark in the most positive way for themselves, their communities, and even the world at large?

Before you can make your mark you must "take your mark," and that's something that champions truly *own*. In this book, I'll use two definitions of champion that you can master to produce peak performances, boldly take the lead, and set yourself and your team up for future success.

And who are these two kinds of champions? They are 1) leaders who stand up for a cause, advocating for others and the greater good, and 2) persons who triumph in life.

The powerful double meaning of champion is woven throughout this book in 11 informative chapters chocked full of entertaining and inspiring stories, and easy-to-implement, practical wisdom.

We'll explore stories full of leadership examples from Olympians, Olympic coaches, professional athletes, my executive coaching clients, and my days at Pfizer Pharmaceuticals. There are lessons from my time as an NCAA D1 Head Coach and swimmer, my experience with 9/11 in NYC, and being a *Playboy* magazine model. You'll be fascinated by how Arctic swimmer Lewis Pugh leads at the United Nations, how Olympic coach David Marsh creates culture for his teams, and how Michael Phelps' coach, Bob Bowman, almost quit coaching. It's going to be interesting and informative, *I promise*.

We'll look at what makes the athlete that may not be the physically strongest still take the gold. And in life, **what makes the unlikely person rise to the top of their profession or lead others to victory?**

We'll cover **10 practical ways to help you** develop leadership skills, habits, mindsets, and traits of champions—borrowed from the best of the world of athletics, corporate America, and life. We'll first discuss how to lead yourself, and then inevitably—and often equally rewarding—how to lead others. The bonus chapter, *Championing Women Leaders*, contains additional motivating stories.

My passion for studying peak performers and leaders started when I was 20 years old, and I've been living leadership every day since then. Besides my experiences mentioned above, I've built and own a multi-million-dollar real estate business, and have been co-founder and president of an international charity.

Most recently and most powerfully, as a journalist who hosts the weekly award-winning podcast, *Champion's Mojo*, I've also gotten access to the secrets of champions through in-depth interviews with Olympians, Olympic coaches, journalists, celebrities, physicians, and other inspiring experts.

It's my observation that people make the biggest transformations and achievements when they change their identities and feel they become "that person who, for example...

...gets up and exercises first thing in the morning."

...speaks confidently in front of groups."

...does the hard things with a positive attitude."

With this book, you'll also learn many other ways to become exactly who you aspire to be. **You may notice the creative chapter titles that embody the type of person that has champion traits**, like the *Eager Leader, Target Maker, Vibrant Visionary, Discipline Developer, Passionate Persister, Habit Hacker, Peak Performer, Confidence Carrier, Reflective Thinker,* and *Success Celebrator.* Through these personas, you will pick up the tools you need to help you become the champion of your own life as well as a strong leader.

At the end of each chapter, you'll find an action area entitled "Lead Yourself" and "Lead Others," along with a convenient summary, to inspire you to achieve your dreams and encourage others to do the same. And among the very last pages of the book is a discussion guide for you to use with your work team, family, or book club to spark conversations that will help take your learning to an even higher level. Now, *Take Your Mark* and let's dive deeper to master the *10 Ways to Lead Yourself and Others like a Champion.*

1

EAGER LEADER

*Eager leaders act caringly with accountability,
confidence, and competence to recognize and fill a need.*

*"A true leader has the confidence to stand alone,
the courage to make tough decisions, and the compassion
to listen to the needs of others. They do not set out to be
a leader, but become one by the quality of their actions
and the integrity of their intent."*

—Douglas McArthur, American General

Crisis on the 36th Floor and Beyond

One of the many things the Coronavirus pandemic has taught us is how vital it is to have great leaders in times of crisis. I learned about this firsthand on the day the Twin Towers were destroyed in New York City.

During my decade of working for Pfizer Pharmaceuticals, one of the many positions I held was as a writer for the company's magazine, *The Force*. Additionally, I was solely in charge of hosting a recorded audio show called *Drive Time*. Both of these were produced for the benefit of informing and motivating the more than 12,000 members of the sales force selling Pfizer's drugs. For two years I was stationed in NYC at company headquarters as a Senior Manager of Communications. This role allowed me access and interviews with the executive management team of this *Fortune* 100 company, where I learned about leadership up close.

On that infamous day, September 11th, 2001, I remember feeling happy as I walked to work in my freshly dry-cleaned chartreuse Liz Claiborne business suit, pearls, tan pumps, and hose. It was also a 'good hair day,' I noted with pleasure. I loved living and working in NYC, and like many people in Manhattan on that exceptionally beautiful, crisp, clear late summer morning, I had a spring in my step. I was also excitedly anticipating the next day, September 12th, my birthday.

The route I covered from my apartment to my office took me by a charming old firehouse with giant open garage doors, shiny red trucks, and handsome firefighters who waved at me every morning while sitting at a round table, drinking coffee as they started their shift. Seeing these smiling men in uniform was one of the highlights of my morning, bipedal commute. My office was located on 42nd Street, on the 36th floor of one of Pfizer's buildings, our global headquarters in the heart of Midtown Manhattan.

I had a job I loved at Pfizer, bright co-workers, and I thrived on the energy of the amazing city and all it had to offer. Life was good. I felt deep gratitude to be living one version of my dream life. I was smiling at people on the way to work, which is not always a common practice in NYC, but on that gorgeous day I was doing it anyway. Little did I know that in just a couple of hours I would be carrying my pumps and wearing holes in the bottom of my stockings as I ran down endless flights of stairs in a terror-filled getaway. That would be the beginning of a 16-hour saga of escaping the war zone that NYC became that day.

I often feel guilty about mentioning any of my own sadness, grief, anxiety, confusion, or pain which I experienced on 9/11. It feels as though it should be insignificant compared to the many who had worked at the Twin Towers, lost their lives, or a loved one. Yet my experiences, memories, and emotions of that event run so deep that, to this day, if I see images of the planes hitting the towers, I am rocked with immediate tears and flashes of feelings that still haunt me.

As I was sitting at my desk around 8:45 that morning, a co-worker popped his head into my office and said, "Hey, come to the back window! A plane just hit one of the Twin Towers and you can see it perfectly." Initially, my mind conjured up a two-person Piper Cub just scratching the facade of the mighty tower. When I turned the corner of the hall to our big picture window facing south, however, I was not prepared for what I saw. The clear day with low humidity provided a direct, flawless view of the towers from our 36th-floor sight-line. There were no buildings tall enough to interfere with our view.

What we saw made the TV images look meek. The plumes of red, orange, and yellow flames and thick black smoke pouring from a gaping hole in the tower were unforgettable and horrific against the brilliant blue sky. This was no Piper Cub. A giant aircraft had hit the tower, and the tragedy and loss of life was obvious. *BAM! Oh my God!* Just as we watched the first tower burning, it was surreal to see a second plane slam into the other tower directly in our view. Not on TV, but live before my very eyes. This could not be real. Was I having a nightmare? Was this war?

Absolute fear and confusion struck many of us when the second plane hit. A wave of nausea came over me. One of my male co-workers, whom I particularly admired, vomited in the nearest trash can. I felt like doing that too, but didn't have enough breakfast in me to produce it. At this point time felt both fast and slow. Several of us stood frozen, watching ghastly clouds of blackness and flames rise into the sky. There was some nervous shrieking in the background. What we thought was debris falling from the towers, we later realized were people jumping from their offices. Though I never saw the media cover it from this angle, several of us in the city's tall buildings flashed fearfully to Pearl Harbor. We felt like we were in a war zone. Would there be more planes flying into the city, crashing into buildings? Many of us were on the verge of panic and wanted to run. I could already smell our sweat mixed in with our fear.

This is when our leader, my boss, Everton Cranston behaved like a real champion. A champion for keeping us safe. I hope none of us are ever put in a situation where we have to replicate what he did, but if we are, this example of Everton's courage is to be kept top of mind. A veritable eager leader, he confidently stepped up to his role and quickly made some tough, unprecedented decisions, always keeping his team's safety and wellbeing at heart.

He called the dozen or so of us in our department together in the conference room. He said, in a decisive, reassuring voice, "We're going to evacuate the building. I need each of you to go to your offices as swiftly as you can and get your personal items, then meet me by the entry door to the staircase." I knew this meant we weren't taking the elevator, and that we'd be hiking down 36 flights. I also knew there was one older woman on our team who would not be capable of making that trek. Everton stayed on the 36th floor with her. He bid us each goodbye and said, "Get to safety, if you can find it. Do whatever you need to do to take care of yourselves." A true eager leader understands their value to their team and enthusiastically embraces that—even in times of crisis. There's a saying that "they walk the talk," which basically means their actions match their words. And competent, confident leaders take those actions earnestly.

As we flew down the stairs, we were shaken by the sounds of emergency evacuation sirens blasting through the halls. It was madness. I ran. So did many others.

Once I hit ground level, I bolted all the way back to my apartment barefoot. Sirens were blaring everywhere and the streets were filled with a parade of fire trucks. The sidewalks were crowded as people rushed to safety. At my apartment I tossed off my suit, ripped off my hose, and got into comfy traveling clothes and running shoes. My plan was to catch a train to Richmond, Virginia. I felt like I was in a war zone and could not "take care of myself" in the city. I threw some stuff into a backpack and went to find my roommate Barb to say goodbye. She was on the roof of our 40-storey tall apartment building watching the inferno surrounding the Twin Towers, along with many other residents. I found her shiny blonde hair among the crowd and told her my plan.

That is when we heard a massive sound and felt the ground tremble. One of the towers was falling. My heart rate had almost returned to normal and my plan to get out of the city had calmed me a bit, but the tremor beneath me now was like another blow. We watched as the first tower fell to the ground in what felt like slow motion. The storm cloud of dust was rising in the sky and I thought it would engulf us, even though we were a safe distance away. We all knew the death toll was rising as we watched. Panic struck me again. I began to run once more. Yes, real sub-8-minute per mile running.

I headed south to Penn Station to catch a train. I passed people covered in white dust heading north. People crying everywhere. Strong men in power suits sobbing into their cell phones. Strangers hugging one another. Emergency vehicles all over the place. The streets were crowded and taxis weren't stopping. The amazing, powerfully positive energy of the city had crashed. When I arrived at Penn Station, I was met by a gruff policeman and barricades. The officer informed me that the station was closed. No trains were running. In fact, he told me that the island, that all of Manhattan was being closed down. No entry or exit. This made me crazy! "What?!" I screamed at him. "I have to get off the island!" Then he mumbled that one of the north bridges might be open. I felt trapped.

There was a bad energy buzzing all around and rumors were flying about the corpses piling up and how the city might become a health hazard. Now my plan was to get to LaGuardia Airport and catch a flight home, not aware yet that all flights had been grounded. I started heading north hoping to find an open bridge. My anxiety was intense and again, I ran. I ran for a few miles and, even though I was a competitive runner, my heart rate was sky-high. Running with a heavy backpack while terrified will do that. I needed a rest so I stopped in Central Park.

I found a bench with only one person on it and plenty of room for me to stop and drink one of the bottles of water I'd packed. I sat down and got control of my breathing. That is when I noticed, in detail, the well-dressed man sitting next to me. At first I noticed just the movement of his body, his shoulders heaving with each crying sob, then I heard his wailing, *wailing*. Maybe me sitting there with him allowed him to release his emotions. Or maybe the reality of the day had just hit him, and he was in pain. I put my hand on top of his and gently asked, "Are you okay?" "No, no," he quietly gurgled through tears. "My best friend was in tower two on the 101st floor. He was above the crash. I know he's dead." "I'm so sorry," I said and began to cry with him. As each moment passed my emotions were getting more raw, and it felt good to let out some of the pressure. My shock and anxiety were now grief for this young man and his friend. I couldn't think about the other massive loss of life that day, or I never would have stopped crying. I felt stuck to the bench, drained of all energy now. But again, as if on cue, I was jolted out of an emotional nightmare by a loud rumbling in the sky.

The rumbling rocked us. Hard to identify at first, but then clearly, it was the sound of a fleet of fighter jets zooming over Central Park and NYC. Everyone in the park looked up, visibly shaken by another assault on our already damaged senses. Fear and adrenaline filled me and the man next to me. We speculated. Were we being attacked? Were those US jets or enemy planes? My negative imagination was now in overdrive. I needed to run again. After a quick farewell to my sad friend, I was off. I walked-jogged many miles until I reached the Triborough Bridge. I went all the way over the bridge to LaGuardia Airport by foot. When I got to the airport I learned that all planes were grounded.

At the Budget Rental Car counter I was lucky to get their last vehicle. The drive to Richmond should have taken eight hours in normal circumstances, but with the required detour around the city and the traffic, it took me 13 hours. Going south on I-95 I passed hundreds of fire trucks heading north to assist NYC in her hour of need. The trucks all had their lights flashing which helped keep me alert as I made the long drive. The procession of endless flashing fire trucks is a unique visual I will always remember. I arrived at my parents' home in Richmond at 2 a.m. on September 12th.

My phone rang the next morning. It was Everton, my boss, my leader. First, he checked on my wellbeing and whereabouts. Then he said, "Happy birthday Kelly." Even in chaos he'd remembered it was my birthday, although I had now completely forgotten. Being considerate and caring is part of being an effective leader. Pfizer leadership allowed us to work from home, "until we felt comfortable" coming back to the city. And this was long before working from home was common. I worked remotely for the next two weeks.

On my first day back in NYC I was happy to be working at the office again. I loved my private, spacious office on the 36th floor, with its big beautiful window and great views of Midtown. As I looked up from my desk, Everton was standing there in my doorway. He said, "Kelly, I want you to stay calm, but please gather your things. I'd like you to work from your apartment here in the city for the rest of the day. We have a possible anthrax threat in the mailroom and we're going to evacuate. But this time you can use the elevators." He smiled and again said, "Do what you need to do to take care of yourself." I went home but was back at work that same afternoon. The anthrax threat turned out to be a false alarm, and after a few weeks, things went back to normal for me at Pfizer HQ.

Madhouse Management: Special Edition

Everton Cranston showed me what it means to be an *Eager Leader*. Not only did he jump at the occasion to take care of his team, but he pulled it off seamlessly in the midst of all of the confusion. Before we break down the key components of champion leaders, let's touch on crisis management as related to the story above and in these unprecedented times of Covid-19. If a leader can manage in times of chaos and crisis, they are more likely to be effective when the storm has passed.

Here are some powerful guidelines that were created by a team of leaders at ghSMART, and published in the *Harvard Business Review*. They found that there are four behaviors that help leaders manage a crisis:

Decide with speed over precision. The situation is changing by the day—even by the hour. The best leaders quickly process available information, rapidly determine what matters most, and make decisions with conviction.

Adapt boldly. Strong leaders get ahead of changing circumstances. They seek input and information from diverse sources, are not afraid to admit what they don't know, and bring in outside expertise when needed.

Reliably deliver. The best leaders take personal ownership in a crisis, even though many challenges and factors lie outside their control. They align team focus, establish new metrics to monitor performance, and create a culture of accountability.

Engage for impact. In times of chaos, no job is more important than taking care of your team. Effective leaders are understanding of their team's circumstances and distractions, but they find ways to engage and motivate, clearly and thoroughly communicating important new goals and information. (Chatterjee, Nichols, & Trendler, 2020; see Notes.)

Pfizer upper management and my own direct boss, Everton Cranston, provided outstanding leadership during the 9/11 crisis. They quickly processed decisions, getting ahead of changing circumstances, accountably acting in their teams' best interests, all while keeping us engaged and motivated with thorough communication. I was grateful for such excellent leadership in one of the scariest times in my life.

Let's Lead!

There seem to be as many different leadership theories as there are letters in the alphabet, and it shouldn't be that complicated. Curating information from top thought leaders and my own experiences, I've identified and broken down the ten attributes, chapter by chapter, that will help make you a **champion leader.** Leading like a champion involves:

- Acting caringly with accountability, confidence, and competence to recognize and fill a need.

- Planning goals that are exciting, specific, measurable, and time-sensitive.

- Practicing in your mind's eye before achieving big goals and sharing a captivating vision to inspire others.

- Using discipline to defeat procrastination, and taking small steps towards your goals to strengthen your discomfort muscle.

- Persisting through pain and discomfort using passion, purpose, positive focus, presence, and preparedness to achieve your objectives.

- Establishing and refining the habits, routines, and rituals that support your physical and mental health and peak performance, and removing those that do not.

- Performing at your best by combating performance anxiety through preparation, routine, and a focus on your own individual mindset.

- Carrying yourself with confidence by developing a strong inner voice to power a can-do mindset.

- Reflecting comprehensively on your experiences to see how you have grown, and how you can improve your life and the lives of others.

- Celebrating all successes, even the small ones, to release stress and increase motivation by imagining a well-earned reward. Celebration involves remembering your strengths, and appreciating and honoring yourself and others.

Integrate these ten points to first champion yourself, then your team, organization, or group.

Learn, Then Lead

Eager Leaders are those who understand that leadership starts with one's self. They aspire to become the best person they can be, and know that before they can lead others, they must be able to lead themselves. Leaders are accountable for their own development. You may have heard the saying, "Leaders are readers," which can also mean that leaders are *learners*. By focusing on developing the ten leading characteristics of champions, you, too, can achieve your dreams and help others achieve theirs. Once you have mastered yourself, it is easier to lead others. Leaders fill a need—they are eager to do the right thing for themselves and to help the greater good. They must be steadfast in their principles and values and continually make learning a priority.

Start with People

The best leaders know that everything starts with people. You can't be a leader without others. Influencing others begins by connecting, and in order to do that, you must take an interest in them. Be a people person. Remember people's names, smile, and look them in the eyes. Greet them as if you are happy to see them. Be genuine. Listen when they speak and make an effort to truly understand them. Show people you care by helping them get what they want and they will want to follow you.

Here's a quick story from my time as a coach at the University of South Carolina. I always tried to recruit the highest-ranked swimmers and was often turned down by them. One evening I was talking with a real blue-chipper, who was fast enough to get a scholarship to any of the top-five swim schools, which we were clearly not. She was keen on attending one of those schools in particular, and therefore not interested in taking one of the recruiting trips to USC. But she told me that she hadn't yet heard from the coach of her number one choice. That coach was a friend of mine, so I said that I'd be happy to call him and make that connection for her. She could not believe I would do that, but I did. A few days later, I got a call from that recruit and she said, "Coach, after you were so willing to help me get what I wanted, I decided you were the kind of person I want to swim for." By simply trying to look out for her best interest, I was able to recruit this first-rate swimmer, who became one of the pillars of our swimming program.

Here's another anecdote from my days selling for Pfizer, which at that time was ranked as the number one pharmaceutical company in the world. There was a reason for this. The techniques Pfizer taught us got us through many doctors' doors, into hallowed hospital corridors, and into the hearts and minds of those we were trying to sell our products to. These extremely valuable people skills from those days have stuck with me. First, if you need to discuss business with someone, start with a focus on relationship and finish with relationship, placing the task in between. At Pfizer we called this R-T-R, relationship-task-relationship, or the *task sandwich*. This works great outside the business world as well. Try it on a friend, or your spouse. *Hey honey, I'm so happy to see you. How's your day going? Would you mind talking with the neighbor about the yard sale before dinner? I'm really looking forward to spending some quality time with you tonight.* Think of how differently your spouse might feel if you charged at them with *just* a task.

Another effective practice for powering up your people skills is to treat *everyone* in an organization as you would the CEO. This includes everyone from the janitor to the C-suite, and all those in between. This was something we practiced in Pfizer, but I've also heard many exemplary leaders tout this as a valuable approach.

Having excellent people skills will make you a better leader. This list includes social skills seen in most admirable leaders, yet if this is an area into which you would like to dig deeper, it's hard to beat Dale Carnegie's classic book, *How to Win Friends and Influence People*. **Remember, no one cares how much you know, until they know how much you care.**

Create a Culture

Creating a winning culture is key to your success as a leader. The culture of a group, team, or organization is defined by its values, traditions, norms, goals, communication style, and leadership from above and within.

Leading others is best achieved by creating a culture that will help ensure the results that you want can be replicated; this is according to one of the most internationally respected and legendary swim coaches of our time, 2016 US Olympic Women's Head Coach David Marsh. David is a master of creating winning cultures. He took over a sub-par team at Auburn University and turned it into a national powerhouse. When I asked David how he'd accomplished that, he said, "Our staff was vigilant in making sure that team members were committed. We had to go into the college bars occasionally and send some people home. I put a freshman in charge as captain because he was the only one I felt represented where we wanted the team to go. I informed everyone that I was only going to accept attitudes that would move us forward and that could see a winning future." And it paid off. While he was the head coach at Auburn, Marsh led the men's team to seven NCAA championship titles and the women's team to five of the same.

David feels that "culture is the centerpiece of a team." Under his leadership, the 2016 US women's Olympic swim team was the winningest in history. He went on to say, "It's better to start with culture and build it slowly than to have a good immediate result the wrong way. Culture will cause the result to repeat." David says two books that have influenced him are *The Culture Code* and *The Talent Code*, both by Daniel Coyle.

Share Your Knowledge

Besides culture, Marsh is a mentor to some of the country's best coaches and swimmers. He's coached over 50 Olympians. In my interviews with almost 100 champion swimmers and coaches, the number of people who mention David Marsh's name as contributing to their success is astounding. He's proof that you can lead others one-on-one and make a huge impact.

I met David Marsh in 1990, while he was at Auburn and I was coaching at South Carolina, both in the same conference. David has always been eager to help and lead others. In observing his eager leadership style through the decades, I've watched him build a huge community of people that he has mentored and led, swimmers and coaches alike, *including me*. He's built his outstanding reputation as a confident, competent leader, brick by brick, one relationship at a time. Creating a culture is a highly effective way to succeed as a leader.

You'll also find many examples in this book from other champions who mention mentoring one another. Leaders share.

Take the Macro View, Then The Micro View

Outstanding leaders look at what's best for the greater good. They understand that a real win is when everyone wins. That being said, they also do everything they can to take individual responsibility for their personal role in a successful outcome. When leaders do this, it is the best possible way of role-modeling accountability and the behavior that will help the cause.

Be Honest

Leaders don't know everything, and often it is best to 'fess up and say, "I'm not sure," or "I could've done that better." Being a leader doesn't mean you are perfect. Permit yourself—and others—to make mistakes. This is very relatable for those with whom you are working, and is actually an effective way to build trust, rapport, and accountability.

Watch Your Words

Do you really hold yourself accountable? What you say to yourself and others about the task you are taking on plays a major role in the outcome. When you really *own* something, your language will convey that. Value this ownership and it will create trust between you and the people around you. Even the tone and attitude of your language can convey accountability and action. One example of this is when taking ownership of a job. If it was a team effort then say, "We did this," but if the work was all yours, then go ahead and exclaim, "I did this!" Another pronoun-related tip that makes people feel included in group conversations is to respond to questions with "Tell us," rather than "Tell me."

Correct As You Go

This is an action of champions. If you realize you are off course, then own that and don't blame anyone but yourself. Accepting to get a job done means taking responsibility for that job. It's perfectly normal to make a wrong turn, in all aspects of life, but acknowledge it then take concrete actions to get back on track. Champions learn to try and try again until they succeed, and it's absolutely fine to ask for assistance along the way.

Put it All on the Line

As a leader, if you fear putting it all on the line, taking on the job, or making a mistake, you might shy away from accountability. Leading requires risk and stepping up to the plate. Making hard decisions and acting when others don't is a large part of leadership. If things don't turn out for the best, you still take responsibility and own the result. But the happy flip side of this is that if things turn out winningly because of your leadership, then you get to own those results too.

Take Your Mark, LEAD!

Lead Yourself

To lead yourself in a crisis begin with your breathing. Breathing affects your nervous system and can provide soothing calm and clarity of mind. **This is a breathing technique that can create calm in both high-stress and everyday situations.** It has been around for ages, probably because it's effective, and I call it the 4-4-8. Let's try it. First, close your eyes. Take a slow deep breath in through your nose for 4 seconds, hold that breath for a count of 4 seconds, and then slowly exhale through your mouth, pursing your lips while making a continuous, light whooshing sound, to the count of 8 seconds. Imagine during that exhale that all stress is leaving you. If you do that two or three times, it works beautifully to keep panic from setting in.

Whether you are in a crisis or not, remain open to communicating with those around you and acting decisively. Observe if there is a need that will serve the greater good—and evaluate if anyone else is willing or able to serve that need. Then take the risk. Feel the fear and do it anyway. Bring out your *Eager Leader* persona and step up to take on the challenge. Not only will it benefit others, but it will benefit you in ways you might not be able to foresee. At first you may not feel eager, but as you develop the other traits discussed in this book, it will become more natural, and your confidence will grow. And remember... *Eager Leaders* act caringly with accountability, confidence, and competence to recognize and fill a need.

Lead Others

We've talked about what leaders do in turmoil, but what about during day-to-day operations? It's all about setting up the ground rules and creating a winning culture. And leaders are continually educating themselves on the latest strategies for success.

That's why they need proven tools to help them. In Pfizer we used the DISC theory, researched by Dr. William Moulton Marston at Harvard University. DISC is a method of identifying predictable actions and personality traits within human behavior. The acronym stands for the four personality DISC styles: Dominance, Influence, Steadiness, Conscientiousness. It can be valuable in raising the productivity of a team or organization. (Auten, Gordon, Gordon, & Rook, 2019; see Notes.)

By connecting to each of the leader personas and tools in the ten chapters of this book, you will make strides in doing just that. I try to read one leadership book per month. Two of my favorites are *Shackleton's Way* by Margot Morrell and *Extreme Ownership* by Jocko Willink. To be a champion leader, be a champion reader.

To be a champion *Eager Leader*:

☑ Learn, then lead

☑ Start with people

☑ Create a culture

☑ Take the macro vs. the micro view

☑ Be honest

☑ Watch your words

☑ Correct your course

☑ Put it all on the line

☑ Use assessment tools like DISC

2

TARGET MAKER

Target Makers plan goals that are exciting, specific, measurable, and time-sensitive.

"Having goals is really important, but so is being flexible in how to reach them. There can be many creative ways to arrive at the same destination."

—Teri McKeever, 2012 Head US Olympic and current University of California, Berkeley Women's Swim Coach

Swimming through Breast Cancer

Having swimming goals saved my sanity and helped me survive cancer. How could I have known that while I was winning four national titles at the 2016 Masters Long Course Championships in Portland, Oregon, I had a tumor growing in my breast? I felt fantastic! I was focused and swimming fast. It was a couple of days before the meet, when I was trying on my skin-tight technical swimsuit that I felt a knot in my left breast as I pulled my suit up over my shoulder. This was mid-August. I pushed out of my mind the thought that it could be anything other than a benign fibroadenoma, which athletes with "dense" breasts often get. I couldn't think about this now and would examine it more closely after the meet. Autumn arrived and, after a summer of fun and activities, I finally attended to the lump. No one in my family had ever been diagnosed with breast cancer, so I thought there was no way the lump could be cancerous. I'd previously had a couple of lumps that were biopsied and turned out to be benign; I was sure this lump would have the same outcome. After a mammogram and two ultrasounds confirmed the existence of this new lump, the radiologist who read my mammogram, Dr. Tsz Ng (pronounced Dr. Chee Ing), wanted a biopsy. Dr. Ng is an easygoing, jovial doctor whom I always enjoyed seeing. And while I hated having a needle stuck in my breast, he and his pleasant staff made the biopsies much more tolerable. As the nurse checked me out after the procedure, she told me to ice my breast, and that they would call me in two days with the results.

Historically, I'd received a few calls from members of Dr. Ng's staff, but never from the doctor himself. **So when my cell phone rang two days later and I heard Dr. Ng's voice on the line, I felt my stomach drop.** "Dr. Ng, I didn't expect to hear from you personally. Is your staff all out sick today?" I joked, trying to lighten the load of anything negative that might be coming. "Kelly, I'm sorry to report that your biopsy came back with results we need to talk about. Could you please come to my office this afternoon so I can give you more details?" Filled with worry, I don't remember Mark, my husband, driving me to meet the doctor. I do remember trying to stay positive and thinking, *Maybe "results we need to talk about" isn't anything that bad.*

In his brightly lit office, Dr. Ng told me, "You have an invasive ductal carcinoma." I couldn't even grasp it. What's that? Is that breast cancer?
Yes.

It was breast cancer. I was diagnosed with breast cancer on October 27th, 2016. At that moment, although I was worried about the future, I knew I'd better set some serious goal lines.

Simplify Goal Setting

The truth about goal setting is that it shouldn't be that complicated. As a leader, being a *Target Maker* for your organization is one of your duties. Clear, concise goals make it more likely that followers can understand and act upon them. It's the same for us as individuals. While it's important that goals are exciting or challenging, specific, and time-sensitive, I also believe that there can be many creative and different ways to reach your target. In this chapter, we're going to focus on what I see most champions doing to achieve their goals. And in reality, utilizing the ten different approaches to success broken down in each chapter of this book will assist you in reaching your destinations.

Target a Massive Goal

So, you've got a huge goal. That's great, because the bigger the better for creating energy and excitement! You want some of your goals to be so compelling that you can't wait to get out of bed each morning and tackle them.

It could be a goal that you've chosen yourself, or it could be something that life throws at you, like overcoming breast cancer. I had set huge swimming goals for this particular season because I had just "aged up" into a new age-group and that's when you are at your best. I didn't want breast cancer to get in the way of my carefully planned swim season. *Heck no, not going to happen!* As it turned out, having these goals was a superb way to keep my mind focused and survive.

Many people have asked me to share my story to bring hope to others. My breast cancer surgery to remove an invasive ductal carcinoma lump, a second (larger) benign lump, and three of the lymph nodes in my armpit took place on Wednesday, November 16th, 2016. I was relieved to have the surgery behind me and to wake up feeling relatively good in the post-op recovery room. My surgeon, Dr. Charles Cox, whom I adored and reminded me of Santa Claus, came in to check on me and asked, "Do you know how to swim?" I thought he was joking with me, but then I realized he didn't know I was a swimmer. I told him that yes, I did, indeed, know how to swim. "Good," he said, "because swimming is an ideal rehabilitation exercise after breast cancer surgery, and helps patients lower the risks of lymphedema." Then he told me I could swim after spending 2–3 weeks out of the water. I took 2.5 weeks off to recover and gently returned to practice on Monday, December 5th. I built my way back slowly, at first just cruising the water, then incrementally increasing my intensity and duration. I was worried about opening up my scar so I didn't stretch my stroke all the way out. Eventually, though, I was back to my old self.

One month to the day after my surgery I swam in the Rowdy Gaines Masters Classic. On the first day of the meet, I swam the #1 time in my age-group for the nation ranked by the United States Masters Swimming (USMS). During the rest of the meet, I swam two other USMS #1 times and set four zone records. I also won the High Point Award for my age-group.

I'm sharing these accomplishments to demonstrate how having very specific goals will help you overcome obstacles. I knew the exact times I wanted to swim—long before the disruption of cancer and surgery hit me—and I swam those times that day. Having clear step-by-step objectives will make it easier to attain them, even when you're faced with hurdles along the way.

Let's talk more specifically about how to break down massive goals into tiny, bite-sized steps. This will help you achieve things that may initially feel overwhelming. Some big goals seem just too big, but there are proven ways to approach them—and many ways to describe that process:

- You can eat a whole elephant one bite at a time

- Baby steps

- The next right thing

- Break it down

Before we continue, be careful who you talk to about your massive goals. Not everyone may *think big* like you do, so save yourself from potential negative feedback from those who don't share your vision. Only tell those who will empower you to achieve your goals.

Bite off Small Pieces

In today's society, we all have a lot on our plates, and sometimes it can become overwhelming. And while I am a true believer in having a strong mindset and envisioning yourself having completed your goal, to get there, you sometimes need to take your eyes *off* the destination. You need to focus on taking baby steps.

Mom's Museum

When my Mom passed away in the spring of 2018, I had to clean out her rather large single-family home. We called it "the museum." Even though she never hit hoarder status, and she kept her house quite beautiful, it was full of family history, tons of photos, and objects with a lot of emotions attached to them. After she passed away and my Dad went into assisted living, it fell on me to declutter their place and sell or find a new home for every single item. To do so, I broke the task down into bite-sized pieces.

My usual ability to visualize the end result, in this case a beautifully renovated home for sale, was clouded with grief. I had just lost my precious Mother and was worried about my Dad. I was too down in the dumps to see out of the clutter, but I kept plugging away at it, day after day, for three weeks straight. Some items went to family, much was tossed out, and the rest was donated to charity. Then the cleaners, painters, and landscapers worked their magic. At the end of a hard month of focusing solely on the details, when I finally looked up from the grind, the house was gorgeous and sold for a fair price. It had all worked out— and it will for you, too, if you just break whatever you need to do into bite-sized pieces. I truly love the metaphor that you can eat a whole elephant one bite at a time. It's such a dynamic visual for having something huge on your plate, yet knowing that with small pieces you could manage the whole thing.

Partner with Someone You Respect

In hitting your goals, it can be paramount to find someone to help you on your way. This could be a formal coach, a role model, a friend. As you know from the beginning of this chapter, breast cancer was a big challenge that was thrown at me, so I found a role model. Arlene Delmage, a swimmer who had recovered from breast cancer and gone on to win many Masters swimming events, was an inspiration and a close friend.

Identify Just the Next Step

I spent the first few days after my diagnosis crying and shaky at the thought of breast cancer. At the time, I was staying at my parents' house because I was helping my Mom who had become very ill with Alzheimer's disease. I couldn't confide in her—she wouldn't have been able to grasp the situation and I didn't want to give her any more grief—and she couldn't support me because her illness had already taken much of her mind.

I locked myself in my parents' guestroom and dialed Arlene's number. "Arlene, I've got breast cancer," I blurted into the phone.

"Okay, okay. You're going to be fine," she said. "Just do the next thing. Do *not* think about anything else. So what's next?"

I said, "I have to get an MRI, and I don't want to get an MRI."

"Honey, it's not painful, just go do your MRI! That's it. Just go do your MRI. And what comes after that?" Arlene asked.

"Well, I think I'll need a biopsy of my lymph nodes."

"Okay," she said, "but we're not thinking about that biopsy yet. Let's just do your MRI first."

So that's what I did. I broke it down into one step at a time. Instead of thinking, *What is this going to look like afterward? Am I going to have a double mastectomy and reconstructive surgery? Is it in my lymph nodes and am I going to die?*

I focused on one thing at a time. First, the MRI. I asked my oldest brother Steve to drive me to my appointment. Steve had experienced many MRIs himself so I knew he would be helpful and supportive. He teased me growing up and used to love torturing me, but on this day he was teasing me just the right amount. He took the day off work to be with me and was loving and fun. We actually had a good time! During my MRI, the nurse said, "Just enjoy whatever you're doing. Stay in that present moment." I remember getting through it and thinking, *Well, that was a piece of cake!* I took each step one at a time from then on.

I was lucky and feel extremely grateful that it all turned out so much better than I could have imagined. I ended up having two lumpectomies, so two lumps were taken out, and these got clean margins, meaning there were no cancerous cells left around the edges of the tumor. They also took out three lymph nodes that didn't have any cancer. Next thing you know, I was back in the pool! Step-by-step-by-step and my cancer experience was done.

Initially, after my diagnosis I'd thought, *Oh my God, my life's over!* And if I had continued to run wild with terrible scenarios, I know it would have been much more painful in all aspects. For me, dealing with cancer became manageable because of the small steps I took, and I am incredibly grateful that my situation was not worse. I realize many peoples' experience with cancer is much more difficult than mine, but no matter how challenging the journey, step-by-step is the only way to get to your goal line. **While we are striving toward a hugely difficult goal, there's an encouraging saying that goes, "Two steps forward and one step backward still gets you to your goal."** There will be setbacks, and we'll cover how to handle those in Chapter 5, *Passionate Persister*.

Take Your Eyes off the Goal

You'll sometimes be hearing about Maria in this book. She's my sister-in-law, my best friend, and my co-host of the *Champion's Mojo* podcast. Maria Parker is a true champion on her bike as well as in life. Our friendship has provided me with such inspiration, wisdom, and support through multiple decades—I'm certain I wouldn't be where I am today without her. She's a world record-holding endurance cyclist and the winner of what is known as the "world's toughest bike race." When it comes to setting and reaching goals, Maria knows her stuff. "Stop thinking about the end. Stop thinking about when you're going to be done. Just do the next right thing," she says. When Maria reviewed an early draft of this section, the title she pitched for it was "How to Achieve Your Goal by Not Looking at It."

Lessons from the Bike

In 2013 Maria won the Race Across America (RAAM). RAAM is an iconic bike race that stretches over 3,000 miles, from California to Maryland. Along the way, cyclists pass through historic landmarks while cycling through deserts and mountain ranges. This is a grueling race, with huge climbs and descents, and extreme temperature changes. **It's been called *hell on two wheels*.** Maria is featured in a documentary film entitled *Hope*, which covers her RAAM journey. Her decision to undertake RAAM in the first place was inspired by facing her sister's terminal cancer, and so fueled by hope, she confronted the impossible in a race she vowed not to quit. When Maria won, she broke the 50–59 recumbent course record, completing the journey in 11 days, 20 hours, and 54 minutes. She was also named the 2013 Female Rookie of the Year.

How did an adult-onset athlete, who came to cycling in her 50s, do this? She broke Race Across America into tiny steps to achieve her big goal of finishing—which turned into winning. I joke that I don't know that I could even make that journey in a car in 11 days. She did it on a bicycle. Maria says, "Finishing that race was probably the highest athletic achievement of my life, and the most difficult. It's a huge goal. Like any huge goal, it was deeply inspiring when I was thinking about it and planning for it. I visualized myself in Annapolis as a victorious rider. I had a very clear and concrete goal. I wanted to finish the race, and I wanted to finish it in a certain number of days. But when I was actually doing it, like so many things, it was much tougher than I anticipated it would be."

I asked Maria to elaborate on some of the details of her RAAM and what made it so tough.

"It's a one-stage race," Maria told me. "After the gun goes off in Oceanside, California, the first person to get to Annapolis wins. What that really means is that anytime you're off the bike because you're sleeping, eating, or taking care of yourself, you're not moving forward. What ends up happening is that you spend a lot of time on the bike, and you become very sleep-deprived. Imagine spending 11 days outside most of the time with very little sleep. Most RAAM racers average less than three or four hours of sleep a night."

Maria continued. "I basically fell apart. Everything fell apart. I was nauseated, throwing up, miserable. I was exercising for 21 hours each day and I couldn't hold down food or water. At one point, I developed asthma from breathing in all the dust in the desert. I was coughing so much that one of my crew members thought I was going to die. Every day I would cry for the first 45 minutes of cycling after my three-hour rest. It became very difficult to go on."

Go Mailbox to Mailbox

Maria said she just did the next right thing. She wouldn't look at the top of the hill she was on. She would go mailbox to mailbox. "I'd be on a country road, and there'd be a mailbox. I'd think, *Alright, I'm not going to think about the goal. I'm just going to get to that mailbox.* I'd cycle to that mailbox. I *knew* I could get to that mailbox. I could see it. I'd get there and feel a sense of accomplishment that would give me the courage to go to the next mailbox, crack in the road, shrub, or whatever it was," Maria told me.

What worked for Maria when feeling overwhelmed in the middle of a long and torturous race was making sure that the next goal was so tiny she *knew* she could do it. She knew she could make it to the next mailbox.

Choose Your Gears

Maria's story inspired a perfect analogy—anyone who's ever ridden a mountain bike up a hill can relate. When you're going up a steep hill, you shift into your tiniest gear which makes it so much easier. It is the same with our goals.

You may think that to achieve your goal you've got to do something hard and be highly disciplined. But the truth is that you can define your targets so that they don't require a massive effort. Just like shifting to the correct gear makes all the difference for a smooth ride.

You can also use tiny gears in stepping your way into leadership positions. Start with something really small. Maybe lead a single meeting, step up for committee chair, or organize the community yard sale. Write your goal down and place it where you can see it in front of you. Small victories lead to bigger victories.

Possibly an even bigger victory than winning the RAAM, is that Maria also champions the cause of raising awareness and money for brain cancer to honor her sister's death. She founded the charity, *3000 Miles to a Cure*. She approached this goal step by step and since 2013 has raised over $800,000 for the cause. Turning your obstacles into triumphs is something champions do.

Think Innovatively

Know that there is often more than one way to hit your target. Part of being successful as a leader is looking at different, sometimes unusual ways to approach your goals. When I talked with Olympic Coach Teri McKeever she said, "I try to be very creative. There's more than one way to skin a cat, and I'm aware of that. I like being innovative and thinking outside the box, and I'm willing to take a chance. I'm willing to say, 'Hey, that was great!' Or, 'Oh, that was stupid, we're not going to do that anymore.'"

Sometimes when you go *far* beyond the box great things can happen, like with world champion swimmer, Michael Andrew, who's now 21. At 14, he skipped the usual path of college swimming and became the youngest professional swimmer in US history. He and his family were scrutinized and sometimes criticized for this unorthodox route. Michael's father, Peter Andrew, is his coach, and he's constantly using innovative techniques to up Michael's game.

Going pro at 14 was just the first step in bucking the system. From their early days as swimmer and coach, the Andrews used an entirely different training technique, known as Ultra Short Race Pace Training (USRPT). This short yardage, high-intensity approach goes completely against the grain of traditional swim training, of slogging through miles and miles and endless hours at the pool.

Michael has broken over 100 National Age Group (NAG) records, multiple Junior World Records, won several national titles as well as a World Championship individual title. He's got a real shot at making the

US Olympic team, but from the perspective of being true leaders and innovators, the Andrew family has already won the gold. From which new angle could you approach your goals that's fresh and divergent?

Create a Vision Board

Target Makers actually spend time looking at their targets. If you are not familiar with vision boards, they are simply a collage of images that portray your goals. Vision boards are my absolute favorite part of making goals and hitting my targets. They are fun and easy to create with magazines, or just by pulling pictures that inspire you from the internet, printing them, and putting them together. Anything that comes to your mind can be depicted with an image.

Think of all the areas of your goals and find a beautiful visual to represent each one. What scenes can you imagine for your ideal health, finances, career, family, home, relationships? Put them all together and look at them every day—you'll quickly see how motivated and powerful that makes you feel! I've used vision boards for decades and they have helped me produce amazing results. I know many champions use them too. Leaders employ them to present a visual for their teams, and you'll find images of ideal products and consumers in the hallways of any successful big company. If you don't want to do a full-blown vision board, you can benefit from the concept and just use separate single images or posters. Did you have any posters on your walls growing up? In my childhood bedroom, I, like thousands of other swimmers, had a big poster of Mark Spitz with seven Olympic gold medals around his neck. This visual inspired me to reach great heights in swimming.

The Pelican Palace

One day during breakfast my husband asked me, "Should we build The Pelican Palace?" Not that long ago, Mark and I owned a vacant ocean-front lot near our home in Florida. It had a somewhat challenging lot shape and location, and before we built on it, we had a hard time deciding if we should construct our home there or sell it. That's when I created a vision board of the exact home that would be best suited for the lot. Once an architect had created the house design, I had an artist draw a fully detailed rendering, including colors, landscaping, a flag flying in front—I even had pelicans flying in the picture! That's how we named it The Pelican Palace. The pictorial showed a four-storey home with oceanfront balconies on every level for watching the frequent satellite and rocket launches from Cape Canaveral. And the architect's drawing included a glass elevator, which was definitely required for our elderly family members. After we saw the image, it was clear to us how magnificent a new home on our lot could be, so we decided to go for it. Building a home on the oceanfront can be a long, arduous process, but having that detailed, full-color rendering kept us motivated and inspired through many tough times. Because we had been able to visualize our end goal, to really see it and even hear the birds flying around it, The Pelican Palace became a reality. What can you create a rendering of in your life to help bring it to fruition?

Take Your Mark, LEAD!

Lead Yourself

Target your most massive goal first. Break down the actions needed to achieve it into small chunks. Find a coach or role model to help you, and at every crossroad, identify just the next step. When the journey to your goal starts to become exhausting, take your eyes off the big picture and focus on the minute-to-minute details. The rest will take care of itself. Create a vision board and put it in a prominent place to keep your goals exciting and front of mind. Only share your goals with positive and empowering people.

On a simple note: I love technology, and while there are some wonderful electronic tools and apps for goal setting, I still believe in the power of putting pen to paper when writing your goals. In fact, I recently bought a brand-new planner. I know it's old school, but somehow I can *feel* things more when I see them in my own handwriting. And remember… *Target Makers* plan goals that are exciting, specific, measurable, and time-sensitive. Maria and I both agree that the best book we've read for helping us achieve our goals has been *Creating Your*

Best Life by Caroline Adams Miller, MAPP, and Dr. Michael B. Frisch. Caroline is a global thought leader on goals and grit, and her books can be instrumental in your success.

Lead Others

When leading others as a *Target Maker*, cultivate creativity and urgency with clear and concise targets. Look for unique ways to solve problems and guide your work team in that direction. Champion leaders also are masters at creating and vividly sharing exciting, specific, measurable, time-sensitive goals for those following. One of my favorite sayings from my days at Pfizer is ***Leadership = Goals + Urgency***. That really rings true when you think of great leadership. It is often someone with a compelling goal that gets things moving quickly in the right direction.

To be a champion *Target Maker*:

- ☑ Simplify goal setting

- ☑ Target a massive goal

- ☑ Bite off small pieces

- ☑ Partner with someone you respect, friend, coach, or role model

- ☑ Identify just the next step

- ☑ Take your eyes off the goal line sometimes

- ☑ Think innovatively

- ☑ Create a vision board

- ☑ Use multiple resources for success

3

VIBRANT VISIONARY

*Vibrant Visionaries practice in their mind's eye
before achieving big goals and share
an exciting vision to inspire others.*

*"Seeing the winning outcome in your mind first
is how to bring about the results you want."*

**—Sergio Lopez Miro, Olympic Medalist,
Coach of Olympic Champion Joseph Schooling**

A Dark Room at the Olympic Training Center

The first time I was introduced to the game-changing life skill of mental rehearsal, using relaxation and visualization, was as a 15-year-old swimmer. I had the good fortune of being selected for an elite distance camp at the Olympic Training Center (OTC) in Colorado Springs, Colorado. When I came back from the camp I put this skill into practice from that day forward.

At that time I was swimming for the Northern Virginia Aquatic Club, which later became Northern Virginia Fun and Fitness, and I swam for Coach John Flanagan. John coached me for over a decade after the elite distance camp. He is now an icon in the swimming world and has coached many national team members and Olympic hopefuls for decades. When I swam for Coach John, he believed in long face-down miles in the pool. Sometimes we logged 20,000 meters in one day! After learning about visualization at the OTC, I would often spend hours and hours focused on the black line at the bottom of the pool, visualizing my goals while I swam.

Now, let's go back to the OTC where our mental training work began. The sports psychologists put us in a dark room. We lay on our backs, they turned off the lights then led us in a relaxation exercise. For the best visualizations, it's ideal to be in a quiet space, maybe a dark place, in a relaxed state—though you can practice them anywhere. We began with deep breathing. Next, they asked us to visualize the outcome of a big race we had coming up. This was how I learned to mentally rehearse for events. I got hooked on it, and soon, I no longer needed a quiet or dark space. I still use visualization throughout my life, both in and out of sports.

Train Your Mind

Research shows **the brain does not know the difference between something vividly imagined and something that you actually did.** (Hamilton, 2019; see Notes.)

A study conducted by Dr. Judd Biasiotto at the University of Chicago showed the power of mental practice. Dr. Biasiotto divided participants into three groups and tested each person on how many basketball free throws they could make. Then he instructed the first group to practice their free throws for one hour daily. He asked the second group only to visualize themselves sinking the free throws. The third group didn't do anything to attempt to improve their throws.

After a month, he tested the participants' free-throwing ability again. The first group had improved by 24%, while the second group had improved by 23%. The third group did not improve.

Without touching a basketball or breaking a sweat, the second group, the visionaries, had improved nearly as much as the first group, who had practiced for 30 hours.

We all know that we can improve almost anything with practice. What most champion athletes *also* know is that significant improvement in their sport can be done from inside their heads, when they're relaxed with their eyes closed.

Mental practice is an easy and powerful tool we can all use. Too often, people don't take advantage of something so simple that could really affect their life. We can use mental practice to change small, daily habits, and we can also use it to manifest big changes. What could you start visualizing today that you'd like to see in your future?

Rehearse to Change Habits

The longest journey starts with one step forward. Whether you're trying to win an Olympic gold medal or get a college degree, it all begins with one small step. And that one small step can be visualization.

Two Visions of the 4 A.M. Alarm

Getting out of a warm, comfortable bed to go exercise early in the morning is one of life's more difficult duties—especially when you're about to dive into a cold pool.

Whether you're headed to swim practice, out for a run or a bike ride, getting out the door is a challenge. But because I learned about visualization at an early age and have been doing it for a long time, it is natural for me to have two visualizations before I go to sleep.

Let me take you back in time. When I swam for John Flanagan, we hit the water at 5 a.m. so I had to wake up to the 4 a.m. alarm. The drive from my house to the pool was 25 minutes, so I needed to be leaving my driveway at 4:30 a.m. We didn't have a garage, so in the winter I had to hack the ice off the car windshield before leaving, which meant I needed to be in my driveway by 4:15 a.m.

When I went to sleep, I would always imagine two outcomes. One, that I would get up, brush my teeth, dress quickly, grab my swim bag, a Pop-Tart, and a thermos of hot tea. I'd drive to the pool, listen to the radio, see my friends, and have the endorphin-high of having done a swim practice before school. I'd feel more physically fit and happier that I had moved myself toward my swimming goals. Then I would drive home, already be showered, alert, and excited for the day. I'd even arrive at school early. That was one visualization.

Then there was the other scenario, which I thought about. I'd wake up, warm and comfortable. I'd hit the 4 a.m. alarm, then I'd go back to sleep. A couple of hours later, I'd wake up and be disappointed with myself for having missed practice. I could imagine Coach John and some of my friends admonishing me at the afternoon practice for missing morning workout. Also, in this scenario I'd have to add time into my morning to shower and have breakfast. When I slept in I was usually late for school and arrived in a bad mood. Which mental rehearsal sounds more appealing to you?

If you want to get up and spend an hour meditating every morning, journaling, doing yoga, laundry, or whatever, then **visualize** it in advance. The week before you decide to implement your plan, visualize it every day before you actually put it into action. Richly imagine the joy and pleasure of being the kind of person who does the things you want to do. Mentally rehearsing your positive outcome will inspire you to become *that* person. As we'll see in Sergio's story below, you can also use visualization to improve a bad situation and see yourself healing. It's that powerful.

Sergio Welds Bones

When Sergio woke up in the hospital after a motorcycle accident, he used visualization to get back on track with his goals.

Sergio Lopez Miro, an Olympic medalist swimmer himself and the coach of several Olympians like Joseph Schooling, Ryan Murphy, and Caeleb Dressel, strongly believes in the power of meditation and visualization. When I interviewed Sergio he told me the following story. "I've been doing a lot of visualization since I was a kid. Even as a youngster, I was seeing myself as the best in the world. Then, in 1987 I was driving my motorcycle into Barcelona when I was hit by a car. I was going about 80 miles per hour and woke up five hours later in the hospital with a broken scapula. This was at the beginning of June and I had the European Championships in August, about eight weeks later. I asked the doctor if I was going to be able to compete and he told me, no way! I was going to have to be in a cast for two or three months."

"By the time I was out of the cast, there was going to be a lot of atrophy in the muscles and nerves. I went to a different doctor who said the same thing, but who suggested a different cast that wouldn't cause as much atrophy. That cast would require me to come in once a week. At that point I started doing visualizations of my healing. One of the things I visualized was seeing my scapula being welded back together. I actually pictured a welder with the bright sparks pouring off, fusing my broken bones back together."

"The other thing I envisioned was my best race after I healed. My best time in the 200-meter-long course breaststroke was 2:19, and I was working towards a 2:16.5. I visualized that race. The blocks. Getting the splits that I wanted. Four weeks into recovery, I went in to see my doctor and told him I felt like I was healed. The doctor took an x-ray and said I was fine! I told the swimming federation that I wanted to go to the European Championships. They said if, in two weeks, I was able to swim 2:20 at the regional championships, they'd take me to Europeans. At the regional meet I swam a 2:20. I was allowed to attend the European Championships and went 2:16.51, the exact time I'd been visualizing."

"I've always done visualization, and as a coach I do a lot of it with my swimmers. I have them visualize moving through the pool and controlling their energy. Some of them might think I'm crazy. I think things are a self-fulfilling prophecy. If you see yourself winning, you win!"

A Video for the Wolfpack Women

Stories like Sergio's inspire me to create ways to use visualization to lead myself and others. I'm a proud alum of NC State University, where I swam in college. I've always been an avid supporter of the Wolfpack, and in 2019 was invited by head coach Braden Holloway to facilitate a high-performance retreat for the women's team. Since then, I've taken a more active role in following them, helping motivate and prepare them for meets during their championship seasons. The 2020 NCAAs were to be held at the University of Georgia (UGA), where I interviewed Jack Bauerle in his office three weeks before this event. Jack's beautiful office looks out directly onto the pool deck.

After the interview I made a video recording of the UGA pool, the locker rooms, the area behind the blocks, the starting blocks themselves, and the stands. I put it all in a seven-minute video and posted it on YouTube, privately, for the Wolfpack women's swim team. With this, they could mentally rehearse with specific, realistic details of what the facility would look like. For much of the video, I stood behind the blocks they would start from, so they could picture their victories. Unfortunately, the NCAAs were canceled in 2020 due to safety concerns during the spread of Covid-19. But this is the exact type of activity you can do to help yourself and others envision their success.

Call in All Your Senses

Vibrant Visionaries believe that it's important to put yourself—in your mind or in reality—in the environment where you will perform. If you can't go there, maybe there's a video or a picture, or maybe you can create some of the circumstances that would occur to help you visualize your success. You can imagine big moments like the end of a marathon finish or the final graduation ceremony when you walk across the stage. We have to see those big accomplishments in our mind's eye and mentally rehearse with all five senses. What does it look like? Smell like? Taste like? What can you hear? Can you feel it?

All those sensations, if we can put them into our minds—the more often, the better—can become a reality. Visualization is so effective because the reticular activating system in our brain cannot tell the difference between something that you've actually done and something you've visualized realistically and repeatedly.

How to Visualize

Just like Sergio envisioned a welder fusing together his broken bones, you too can picture the outcomes you want. To help you with this, I'm going to share my favorite visualization exercise. Read through it first to get an idea of how it works, then try it on your own.

Get Comfortable

Find a quiet, dark place where you're not going to be interrupted. Get into a comfortable position. You don't necessarily need to be lying down, and could do this in your car on your lunch hour, or anywhere you're not going to be disturbed.

Breathe in Calm

One of the best ways to relax your mind is by taking big, deep breaths. As we learned in Chapter 1, the *Eager Leader,* proper breathing during a crisis or panic attack can make all the difference in calming us down. This same breathing works perfectly here. First, close your eyes. Take a slow deep breath in through your nose for 4 seconds, hold that breath for a count of 4 seconds, and then slowly exhale through your mouth, pursing your lips while making a continuous, light whooshing sound, to the count of 8 seconds. Imagine during that exhale that all stress is leaving you. If you do that two or three times, that will bring you into a parasympathetic state, which is the relaxation response. That turns off the critter brain, and it will get you into a more creative state of mind. As a side note, this breathing technique is also an effective hack for insomnia. Try it one night when you're tired of counting sheep.

Relax Your Body

Go through your entire body from your feet up, tensing then relaxing each muscle group. Tense your feet and relax your feet. Tense and relax your calves, and so on. Go all the way up through your quads, your hamstrings, your glutes, your abs, your back muscles. Tense and release your fists, your forearms, your arms, your neck. Clench your jaw, release your jaw. If this is too active for you, then simply envision a warm, golden light originating at your feet and moving up your body to your head in a wave of relaxation.

Envision a Peaceful Destination

Mentally bring yourself into a peaceful place. For you, that may be on the edge of a babbling brook in the midst of a cool forest; or walking along the beach at sunset, shallow waves lapping the shore; or relaxing in a hammock in a rich green garden with a koi pond and wind chimes softly ringing. In one of my favorite scenes, I'm watching the morning sun glistening off the ocean that is just turbulent enough to create patterns of shimmering light, like a kaleidoscope. I can hear the soft sloshing of the water as I swim through it. I see myself gliding through this gorgeous element and can smell and taste the salt on my lips and in the air. The shades of transparent blues, blue-grays, and deep black fill my eyes through my goggles as I scan from the surface to the depths. I feel the refreshing, but not cold, waves on my skin, a buoyancy and a slight rolling of my body with the current rising and falling. I feel bliss, joy, ahhh... I'm home.

Create Your Vibrant Vision

Start creating images in your mind's eye. Whatever the situation that you envision, whatever you want, whatever habit you want to create, or outcome you want to see, imagine you are there, in person, in that situation. Just like in the beautiful William Wordsworth poem, *Daffodils*, use your "inward eye."

One of the scenarios that I'm so familiar with is standing behind the starting block at a big competition. Right now, I can particularly envision the University of Minnesota, Jean K. Freeman Aquatic Center.

I'm standing there barefoot. My feet are wet behind the block; I'm waiting behind lane number four, and I can hear the announcer giving the names of the swimmers in the heat before me. I can see all the gigantic aquatic stands, everybody in the stands, and the big scoreboard with the times coming up. I can smell the chlorine. I can still hear the announcer in the background, the splashes behind me in the warm-up pool, and in front of me in the competition pool. Then I hear the double whistle for my heat to step up onto the block. When I step up I can feel that sandy, gritty, swim block under my feet, and I feel the nerves.

My stomach is getting butterflies just writing this.

I visualize grabbing the block and feeling that uncomfortable metal edge under my fingers and my toes. It's very painful, on some blocks, to grip your toes around the edge. I see myself streamlining off the block and having a beautiful, long, slim dive that goes in deep, and several dolphin-kicks before I come up.

I'm not going to take you through my whole race, because I think you get the picture. You need to use all of your senses. I'll fast forward to the end of that race.

I'm dominating my heat. I look up at the scoreboard and see a #1 next to my name. I see the time that I want.

Right now, I swear I feel like I have just swum that race.

Swimming is easy as far as visualization goes because you've got all these rich sensory details that you can put in. But whatever your passion, your goal, your arena, or your habit, find the details to make your visualization feel as real as possible.

My hope is that this guided visualization has given you an aerial view of why mental rehearsal is so important, and why it really works.

Coaches Who Praised

As *Vibrant Visionaries*, if we share the vision we have for someone else, it can lead them forward and on to great things. I was incredibly grateful that I got to swim for many iconic coaches. The first one in my youth was Stan Tinkham, the 1956 US Olympic swim coach for the women's team. I was only ten years old in 1971, when Coach Tinkham made a comment to me that truly upped my level of confidence. In the middle of practice one day Stan called me out of the water and on deck to his side and said, "Kelly, you have a natural, world-class freestyle." I always remembered those words and carried that confidence forward for my entire swimming career.

Another visionary coach I swam for was Don Easterling at NC State University. On this occasion, our women's team was getting on the bus to head to Charlottesville, Virginia to the ACC Championships. The women's meet was the week before the men's meet, so Coach Easterling was staying in Raleigh to coach the men as the women traveled with the other coaches. Coach Easterling saw us off at the bus. Before I boarded he put his arm around my shoulder and whispered in my ear, "I'm sorry I'm not going to be there to watch you, but I know you are going to do amazing things! I've seen how hard you've worked. You are ready. I believe in you. I see you on that podium. Now go make it happen!" When I took my seat on that bus, I embraced the vision that Coach Easterling shared with me and I did, indeed, make it happen. It was the performance of my career, up to that point.

Take Your Mark, LEAD!

Lead Yourself

Practice using visualization for big and small goals. You can picture yourself as a leader. A great way to develop confidence is by doing the task repeatedly in your mind first. We've learned in this chapter that the mind cannot tell the difference between something real and something vividly imagined, so go ahead, imagine yourself succeeding at your goals! You can also imagine two different outcomes to help you choose the better path. No doubt when you master this skill you will put yourself in the best possible place to confidently lead and bring out your inner champion. And remember... *Vibrant Visionaries* practice in their mind's eye before achieving big goals and share an exciting vision to inspire others.

Lead Others

Leaders create the vision of the destination to inspire others. As leaders, if we share the vision we have for someone else, it can lead them forward and on to powerful performances, like in my examples of *Coaches Who Praised*. Be able to articulate the who, what, where, and why of any vision. Tell your team about Dr. Biasiotto's study on how people improved their free throws through mental practice only. Then lead others through a guided visualization. Use what you've learned here to help your team relax and vividly imagine performing at their peak and achieving big goals.

To be a champion *Vibrant Visionary:*

☑ Call in all your senses

☑ Use visualization

☑ Get comfy

☑ Breathe in calm

☑ Relax your body

☑ Envision a peaceful place

☑ Create vibrant visions for yourself and ones to share
with your team

4

DISCIPLINE DEVELOPER

Discipline Developers find meaningful motivation, defeat procrastination, and take small steps in the direction of their goals to strengthen their discomfort muscle.

"Many things I learned in sports, like discipline and time management, carry over to life and the business world for success."

—Cullen Jones, Olympic Champion, First Black World Record-Holding Swimmer

Lewis Swims through Chunks of Ice

Lewis Pugh is a modern-day superhero. The Arctic Ocean freezes at a temperature of 28.8 degrees Fahrenheit, lower than the normal 32 degrees because of its high salt content. So when Lewis swam 1,000 meters at the North Pole in 29.2-degree water, it was liquid with chunks of ice. Most people would never consider a dive into the black, icy waters, but Lewis does such stunts to bring attention to the need to protect our oceans. Lewis is an endurance ice-water swimmer and the United Nations Patron of the Oceans. He is the only person to have completed a long-distance swim in every ocean of the world.

Today he has pioneered more swims around famous landmarks than any other swimmer in history. Each of these seemingly impossible feats was done to raise awareness about the vulnerability of our oceans and their importance to humanity.

He puts his body on the line to get people talking about marine-protected areas, by swimming in sub-freezing temperatures. Online you can see video footage of him swimming through chunks of ice. He also swam 329 miles (528K) in the English Channel over a fifty-day period. And that, too, was in dangerously cold waters.

One of the highlights of my journalistic career was sitting down with Lewis Pugh in Boston, Massachusetts in October 2019, when he was there receiving a humanitarian award. I was surprised when he told me that he was terrified a lot of the time. **"I know I'm undertaking swims which have never been attempted before, and in water that is extremely, extremely cold, literally freezing, 29F or -1.7C degrees.** I'm terrified when I swim in those temperatures, but for me it's all about courage, discipline, and training. I'm good in the cold because I spend a lot of time in the cold. I feel it's important to push yourself into those dangerous places, into places of fear. One can soften up really quickly, and I find when I'm beginning to soften up, I need to jump into very cold water."

Besides the dangerous cold, Lewis admits he's also terrified of the potential predators in the water. "When I'm in South Africa, I go down to a Capetown beach late at night and I swim in the dark, on my own. To normal people that probably sounds absolutely crazy, going swimming in water with great white sharks late at night by yourself. And to be honest, when I'm swimming in the dark, everything looks like a great white shark. Every piece of kelp feels like a great white shark. I can't wait to get out and get back into bed. But after I've done that swim, then I feel confident that I have what it takes to go into even tougher environments. Those tougher environments can be death zones."

"When I'm swimming in Arctic waters, I'm under no illusions of my safety. I know I'm in a death zone. The difference between swimming in cold water and icy Arctic waters is like the difference between walking in the foothills of the Rockies and climbing Mount Everest in the middle of winter. It is quantumly different. It's extremely painful."

"I feel that water grab me as soon as I dive in. I can barely breathe. I'm gasping for air. That water just grips its way around you and holds you like a vise. Every single stroke is very, very difficult. My mind is saying, *Get out of here immediately! You could die!* So you've got to persuade your mind and you've got to have the discipline to stay and convince yourself that actually, you can do this."

Now *that* is discipline. Maybe not the kind that you and I need every day, but it's a significant source of inspiration and demonstration of what the human body can handle, and what the human spirit can achieve.

Decipher Discipline and Defeat Procrastination

Procrastination is the enemy of discipline. In this chapter, you will understand what discipline really is, the science behind procrastination, and the reasons why we do it. You'll learn ways of bringing discipline into your life as well as techniques you can use to overcome procrastination.

On the topic of discipline, I consider Jocko Willink, a retired Navy SEAL, one of the top thought leaders. Jocko says that discipline is freedom—and I agree with him completely. Think of it this way: If you want financial freedom and have the discipline to create income from your side hustle and become an entrepreneur, then you may get the chance to quit your job and have that freedom one day. You could lose weight to free yourself from your pants being too tight, or meditate daily to find freedom from negative thoughts. There are so many other ways of looking at this, too, but one thing is certain: When you're disciplined, you become free and good things happen to you.

Discipline is when your thoughts match your actions. Your inner voice may be saying, "I should go running," "I should meditate," or "I should get up off the couch and finish that project I promised I'd send out by two o'clock." There's always a reason not to practice discipline. But don't let that deter you from the satisfaction and potential rewards that come with accomplishing your goals. Don't procrastinate.

Understand Procrastination

Procrastination is a challenge that we all face at one point or another. Who hasn't struggled with delaying and/or avoiding issues that are important to them? Why do we procrastinate and how can we kick this bad habit for good? Let's dig into the science of procrastination then look at some tools that can help.

I admit it: I can be a procrastinator. And once I started digging into the research on this, I realized that I procrastinate more than I'd like. But why is that so, for many of us?

One book that I love and recommend is *Atomic Habits: An Easy and Proven Way to Build Good Habits and Break Bad Ones* by James Clear. According to Clear, we procrastinate because we are thinking of our present self, yet the thing that we are procrastinating about is going to serve our future self.

We've seen what Lewis Pugh does, which takes incredible discipline and is an exciting, extreme example of such. Then there are the mundane, everyday things that make our lives better but still require discipline, like exercising, for example, or cleaning the house. How many of you have put off doing your taxes, returning important emails, or calling a loved one? Procrastinating as a leader might mean that you have to deliver bad news. You know it needs to be done, but it's a difficult task. Disciplined leaders do the hard things first. My husband Mark, a former Marine Corps officer, shared a saying they have in the Marines. "Bad news doesn't get better with time." Getting hard things done and out of the way always makes you feel better.

Cross the Action Line

In his book, Clear refers to something he calls the Action Line. To me, the word procrastination indicates that the task eventually *does* get done.

However, it doesn't get done when you could give it your best. Think back to your projects in school, for example. Were there times when you had something due on Friday morning that you started working on Thursday night? I bet I'm not the only one who did that! But once you start and cross what's called the action line, you then feel relieved and powerful, like you could actually get it done. You can get addicted to that feeling of crossing the action line, getting a real rush from that waiting-till-the-last-minute stress. But honestly, this never results in your best performance.

Future Fit You

Since exercising is one of the top items we put off, let's use that as an example of Clear's crossing the action line *and* thinking of your future self, combined. The most difficult part of exercise can be just getting started. Once you cross the action line and are moving, though, the endorphins start to flow. Even if you start out by promising yourself *just* five minutes, it almost always turns into more. An additional tool for prompting you to act is thinking of your future self. In this case, exercise is a double win. First, you feel the results on your immediate future self directly after a workout, with your endorphin high and post-workout glow. Then there's an even more futuristic self, weeks and months ahead, that you can think of to inspire and drive you. How great will it feel to be able to wear your favorite jeans again, and to be physically fit and energetic enough to do more of the activities you cherish?

To motivate yourself and stave off procrastination, think about the future self versus the present self. Think of how fulfilled you feel *after* exercising, paying off bills, cleaning your house, or calling someone you love.

Factor out Fear

In general, we shouldn't take or not take actions based on fear. Nelson Mandela said, **"May your choices reflect your hopes, not your fears."** According to research, fear is a major factor in procrastination. (Carlbring & Rozental, 2014; see Notes.) I'm coming up on my fifth anniversary of my breast cancer diagnosis and surgery. One thing I'm supposed to do is to have mammograms every six months as opposed to yearly. Ideally, by now I should have had 8–10 mammograms, however

I've only had two. The reason for this is that when the six-month mark approaches, I find some excuse to get out of it. I'm simply afraid. My youngest brother Jim has always been my protector and close pal. Jim is an accomplished radiologist who has seen too much breast cancer in his career, and he's also a voice in my head. "Kelly, I know you're scared, but if you catch breast cancer early, it is often 100% curable. And even if it's not curable, your outcome will be better the earlier we catch it and treat it," he says. If it were not for Jim, I would probably never do mammograms again.

In talking with other breast cancer survivors, I learned that they feel the same way. My good friend Arlene, the *Target Maker* you met in Chapter 2, also procrastinates when it comes to going for her mammograms. When I asked her when she last went for one, she replied that it had been a couple of years. I knew she was supposed to do it by the end of the summer. She responded that she was going to enjoy summer, travel with her family on vacation, and go in for her mammogram in the fall when her kids went back to school.

I believe she was simply putting it off, probably because she was afraid. I think there's always a little bit of fear when you've had any type of illness. You become fearful of receiving a bad health report.

And it's not necessarily a potentially bad health report you're afraid of. It may be that you're scared to step into a leadership role or try a new approach to a problem. But crossing that action line shuts down procrastination.

Now that we've discussed what discipline and procrastination are about, let's look at the strategies you can use to develop the former and defeat the latter.

Six Ways to Strengthen Your Discipline Muscle

It's one thing to know, in your mind, what you need to be doing to achieve the result you desire. It's another thing to get your actions to match these thoughts. So how do you get your actions and thoughts to align so that you can reach your destination?

There are countless ways to develop discipline, and now we're going to cover six very effective techniques that I've seen champions use. Let's start with the first one of assuming a new identity.

1–Assume a New Identity

One of my favorite quotes is by legendary motivational speaker Denis Waitley, who says, **"It's not who you think you are. It's who you think you are not."**

Assuming a new identity means embracing the identity of the kind of person you want to become. Let's say that you're a meat-eater and all your friends know you as the person who grills every weekend. You decide to adopt a plant-based diet and all of a sudden, you're eating only vegetables and loving it. This means taking on the persona of being a vegetarian, and you might even say the words in your mind, *I'm a vegetarian*. Own your new identity and it will help you embrace your new lifestyle. You have now become that kind of person who loves vegetables.

This works in business and leadership situations too. You can put into action what we've covered in Chapters 1–3, such as knowing what exemplary leaders do, how to target your goals and how to visualize, disciplining yourself to be the person of your deepest desires. The next story is an outstanding illustration of this point.

The Gracious Surgeon

Let me introduce you to a champion of children's health as well as a champion in the swimming pool, Dr. Peter Yu. Pete is a dedicated pediatric general and thoracic surgeon, and an accomplished Masters swimmer. Aside from many larger goals, Pete is working on having the discipline to be consistently nice when his phone rings at 3 a.m.

As one of my current executive coaching clients, Pete allowed me to share this story. In my coaching practice, the-type-of-person-who-exercises is a tool that can truly change behaviors. Pete made a break-through the other day during one of our sessions on this topic.

As a surgeon on-call, he gets night calls at all hours. When awakened, Pete says he can sometimes be brusque. He does not want to be grumpy to the person on the other end of the phone, and told me he wants to be gracious. At first he said that he was going to say to himself, *be gracious*, right before he answered the call. This can be an effective reminder-cue, which works temporarily and urgently. Then we discussed that he really is a gracious person, and he said, "Yes, it would be more powerful to tell myself, *I'm a gracious person*, or, *I'm the kind of person who is gracious, even when I get a phone call in the middle of the night.*"

Pete continued. "I've long felt it exhausting to *be* someone I am not. It's too tiring to not be yourself. And eventually, there will be failure because you can't keep up a facade. But as a counter-principle, I realize I am gracious in countless other settings. I'm gracious with my wife, my patients, my bosses, my friends, my swim teammates. So it's easier to draw on that, to realize I already have that skill, I already am that person, and just 'slide' or transition it over to night calls. The mantra or hack of repeating to myself that I am gracious is just a reminder to do so."

Play around with Pete's technique if you are trying to take on a persona in one area that you may not be strong in. Just "slide" it over from a part of you where it already works. This can help you assume that identity more authentically.

Here's another powerful example that might help if you are trying to quit smoking, drinking, or biting your nails, for example. If someone offers you a cigarette and you are *not* a smoker, you are going to say, "No thank you, I'm not a smoker." But what if someone offers a cigarette to a smoker who is on their third day of trying to quit? If it's Wednesday and their friends don't know that they quit last Sunday, they may say, "No, thank you," when offered a cigarette. They may even say, "I'm trying to quit."

But what if they said, "I'm not a smoker"? All of a sudden they've owned that they are not a smoker. That's powerful and self-motivating. Think of those identities that you want to identify with and where you're going. Where are those thoughts taking you? What are the goals? When you achieve that goal, *who* will you become? I love the concept of *fake it till you make it*. At first, you may have to work at being that new person, but at some point you will cross the line into authentically being that person.

2–Find Your Why

Why does Lewis Pugh dive in in places like the North Pole and complete endurance swims in below-freezing water temperatures? He says he is motivated by his "driving purpose," his why, which is saving our oceans.

Why is it that you want to have discipline? What's your big goal? A big hairy, audacious goal, or BHAG, is a clear and compelling target for motivation and excitement. The term BHAG was coined in the book *Built to Last: Successful Habits of Visionary Companies* by Jim Collins and Jerry Porras. What is the one thing that is so motivating to you that you don't even need discipline? You're so motivated that you're up before the alarm clock and out the door, going for it. Whether big or small, that's your why. When you've got your why, you can use Post-It notes or put it on your tech screens to remind you. And if it's not a big, hairy, audacious goal, then maybe it's a mid-sized goal that you need to be reminded of. Maybe it's something that you're doing for someone else. Whatever it is, having a why is huge and will motivate you to push forward.

3–Start Your Day with Difficulty

Taking a cold shower is something that everyone can do to help develop discipline. Cold showers strengthen your discomfort muscle. Research shows that when you do something difficult at the beginning of your day, you have a boost in self-esteem and feel like you can accomplish more tasks. Apart from building your discomfort muscle, cold showers also help create a neural pathway in your brain that confirms you are able to deal with challenges. (Hof, W.; see Notes.)

When you're talking negatively or positively to yourself, you're reinforcing a neural pathway. When you're meditating and your mind snaps away and you bring it back repeatedly, you're developing a sort of muscle, a skill. It's the same way with discomfort.

You've got to ease into cold shower therapy. First, do your normal warm shower to wash your hair and body. When you are done with that, it's time to crank down the heat. Gradually turn the temperature down— it's more difficult to go from super hot to super cold. Use upbeat music to accompany you. Take this time to repeat power mantras like, "I'm strong. I'm powerful. I can do this!" Breathe deeply. Breath changes our being physically and emotionally, so play around to see if deep or shallow breaths work better for you in dealing with the cold. Time yourself. It's motivating to see that you've upped your time in the cold, especially when you know all the benefits of cold exposure.

Step into a Cold Shower or Tub

Cold therapy is anti-inflammatory and antidepressant, and it boosts your mood, immune system, and metabolism. Cold showers also give you more energy and mental clarity, while reducing stress and anxiety. (Shevchuk, 2008; see Notes.) They are also a way to train your discomfort muscle and then transfer that discipline to running, meditating, or whatever you need to do.

Showers are not the only way to benefit from cold therapy. You can use a pool, lake, or even the cold outside air. For inspiration, you may want to research Wim Hof, a thought leader on cold exposure therapy. He says it can be as simple as putting on your bathing suit and running around the house twice in the winter.

Cold showers are very doable and an uncomplicated option when starting your journey into cold therapy. If you live in a warmer climate like me, where the water out of the tap is not very cold, maybe you can take an ice bath instead. Ready to give it a try? Ease your way in and brrrrreathe. You'll be glad you did.

4–Ease into Change

If you are not familiar with the Kaizen theory, it is a valuable tool for making change less painful. Kaizen is a Japanese term that comes from "kai," which means change, and "zen," which means good. Together, they represent "change for the better," or "continuous improvement." The state of Kaizen is an aspiration.

This technique is the opposite of what we discussed earlier, and is about using small motivations to achieve your objectives rather than going after big audacious goals. With Kaizen, discipline doesn't have to be highly uncomfortable or about making massive shifts.

Kaizen is a way to avoid our critter brain. The critter brain wants to keep us safe and doesn't like change or risk, and Kaizen helps us get around that. It's also a way to get around the concern or shame of failure. Let's say you decide that you're going to run a marathon in the next few months. Now that's a daunting goal if you've never done it before! Most people may not want to announce that they are going to run a marathon because they've probably shared a big goal in the past and have failed.

In other words, saying that you are going to go on a morning run may fail to get you out of bed. But if you say that you are just going to go on a one-minute run, then you wouldn't be intimidated. Today, you may go one minute, and tomorrow, you may go two. The next day, you might run three minutes, or ten. What you are doing is slowly building your confidence to do the marathon, and circumventing that lizard brain and fear of failing.

Research shows that this is very effective, but you have to trick your brain incrementally. (Daniel, 2020; see Notes.) Let's go back to the cold shower for a minute. This is another way that people can use Kaizen. You take a cold shower for 10 seconds and then gradually build up to 20 seconds, then 30, and so on until you're up to three minutes and reaping all the benefits. It's not nearly as overwhelming.

After decades of distance swimming, I have to constantly do physical therapy on my worn-out shoulders. I've found what I almost consider to be a miracle cure on the subject, a book entitled *Shoulder Pain? The Solution and Prevention,* written by John M. Kirsch, M.D., an orthopedic surgeon. It is the result of 25 years of research into a new and simple shoulder exercise program to treat and prevent rotator cuff tears, the impingement syndrome, and the "frozen shoulder," which are all too common for swimmers. If you know anyone with shoulder problems, I highly recommend this book.

Based on Dr. Kirsch's advice, I've been doing exercises that help rebuild my shoulders. These involve hanging from a pull-up bar, like ones you can find at fitness centers and children's playgrounds. I have one that you attach over a door frame. When I first started this exercise, I had been diagnosed with a torn rotator cuff and impingement syndrome in my left shoulder and was headed for shoulder surgery. But now hanging has helped me tremendously. The book says to work up to five to ten minutes of hanging a day. At first, I could barely hang on for 20 seconds! But I gradually built up to where I can now hang for at least five minutes, and sometimes I even do two sets of five minutes. Little by little, that's what Kaizen is about.

Discipline is about hitting targets by matching your thoughts to your actions to fulfill your intentions. It works well when you are thinking about things like running, meditating, and writing a book. However, the Kaizen theory is also good for reverse engineering. If, for example, you want to stop a bad habit such as drinking alcohol or overeating, then you can simply reverse it. You can get your normal full plate of food but before you eat, remove one tablespoonful of food from your plate. Grab your beer, but give the first gulp to someone else, pour it down the drain, or leave a little at the bottom of the bottle. Just a little bit more, or less. Kaizen is beneficial for achieving goals—and these include getting rid of habits that you no longer want in your life.

5–Know Your Strengths and Weaknesses

Knowing your strengths and weaknesses is extremely helpful in being disciplined. For example, if you're trying to get out of bed early and you know your weakness is looking at your phone in bed, then you don't want to keep your phone next to your bed. It makes it too easy to spend 15 minutes on social media or checking your emails, delaying your morning. If you know you're supposed to give up junk food, then remove all of it from your home. And don't buy any more! Junk food is a weakness for many people, and if it's easy to access, it's going to be almost impossible to resist. Recognizing your weaknesses, what is going to tempt you, and what's going to delay you, can be tremendously valuable.

You should be able to acknowledge your strengths as well. For example, most experts agree that it's best to exercise in the morning. Willpower tends to be stronger in the morning than in the evening, so that's part of the theory behind this recommendation. But if you enjoy working out in the evening and are motivated to do so, then go ahead and create your own schedule. Maybe you're an evening person and that's your strength. Or maybe you're a great listener so others confide in you easily, or you're good at making people laugh. **Everybody has strengths that make being around them rewarding.**

In a similar vein, if you're good at written communication but are aware that you also have a weakness or tendency to put off difficult, face-to-face conversations, then engage in regular meetings and live interactions with your work team or family. This will allow for a more natural flow of communication, where good and difficult conversations can occur.

Knowing your strengths and weaknesses is a huge key in being successful, especially when coupled with matching your thoughts and actions.

6–Comprehend Your Motivation

What motivates you? This goes beyond knowing your *why*. In executive coaching we call this *the why beneath the why*. Knowing your motivation means understanding the deeper emotions driving you. So what's your driving factor? Is it fear? Is it finances? Is it excellent health? I'll share another story from one of my executive coaching clients who allowed me to use her first name only. Let's meet Virginia. Virginia wanted to be the lead on an upcoming company project because she thought she had more expertise than anyone else in the group. However, she was hesitant to speak to the higher-ups and request that she be in charge. "I'm not sure if I want the extra hours and responsibilities," she admitted. Then I asked her if she could go deeper, to drill down further, to really find out why she wanted to lead this project, setting aside the fact that she was an expert on the topic. She said, "I guess if I really think about it, I failed at a similar project in my last place of work, and that made me feel self-conscious and unappreciated. I know I'm able to master a project like this now because I'm a lot more experienced. I want to do this to build my confidence and I know when I do an excellent job at it, I'll be and feel appreciated." I asked her if this felt like a more compelling reason to go and request to lead this project. She said it definitely did. "Now I feel excited about it, and I don't even mind the extra hours or responsibility. That was just an excuse," Virginia added.

In the end, Virginia took the lead on this project and achieved not only success but feelings of recognition and confidence. By drilling down to a deeper layer to uncover *the why beneath the why*, you are more apt to motivate yourself and those you are leading. Find your motivation and the emotion attached to your why.

Four Tools for Power Over Procrastination

Benjamin Franklin wrote, "You may delay, but time will not, and lost time is never found again." Here are four tools for defeating procrastination so that you don't have to lose time. These tools are simple but effective, and you can start using them immediately.

1–Use Temptation Bundling

This is a technique that was researched and developed by a behavioral economist named Katy Milkman at the University of Pennsylvania. (Milkman, Minson, & Volpp, 2013; see Notes.) She found that if you bundle things that you are fearful of or don't enjoy doing together with things that you like, you're more likely to get them done. For example, if you don't like to exercise, then tell yourself you're only allowed to listen to your favorite podcast or audiobook while riding a stationary bike. Tell yourself that you can only get a pedicure while you review all your old emails, or you can only watch your favorite TV show while folding laundry.

I've received a lot of feedback that people love our one-hour podcast format for *Champion's Mojo* because they can go running or walking for one hour as they take in an episode. This is certainly better than accomplishing nothing while listening to a podcast!

Here's Katy Milkman's theory of temptation bundling in action. My niece, Erika, is a doctor and we don't get to visit much because we live in different cities. Recently, Erika was visiting during the same time as I had a mammogram scheduled. We've already established that as a breast cancer survivor, these appointments are hard for me. The reassurance of having a doctor and a niece I love with me sounded like a perfect way to wrap a visit with Erika and my dreaded exam together, so I called her. "Hey, Erika, come with me to my mammogram because there's a lot of sitting around and it's a 45-minute drive each way. We'll get a few hours together to catch up and I'd love your emotional support as well." Erika was happy to do it. This is one example of bundling something unpleasant with something pleasant. A win-win.

When you are temptation bundling, think of something that you don't want to do and ask yourself what joyful activity you can partner it with. Don't think of it as if you're taking your favorite pedicure and ruining it by going through your emails. Treating yourself to something nice will increase your discipline to do something difficult.

2–Make a Commitment Contract

A commitment contract is an agreement you sign with yourself to follow through with your intention. Sometimes making a commitment will help increase your discipline. There are many tools online to help you stick with your goals. One I like is at *stickk.com*. It's for anyone who has a big task and wants to commit with some accountability. The Stickk strategy works by using the psychological power of loss aversion and accountability to drive behavior change. You put your money on the line in case you fail to live up to your commitment contract.

For example, I have another book I'm writing for which I've written about six out of 12 chapters. I have the remaining chapter outlines prepared and I want to finish the book fairly quickly, without too much procrastination. The way I would use this strategy is to first decide that I'm going to have the manuscript done by December 31st. Then I would sign up on *stickk.com* and put up $100 as collateral that I'm going to have the book done by that deadline. If I don't meet the target, that $100 goes to a designated charity. Choose an amount that motivates you. This is a cool way to get yourself going.

Stickk.com is a tech tool, but if you don't want to involve technology, there's also a simpler way to make a commitment contract. Write out the commitment you want to make, being as specific and focused as possible with your actions and deadlines. Use formal language so you see it as a legitimate agreement. Make sure you put in the reward for accomplishing it as well as the consequences if you do not, which could include making a monetary contribution to a charity, for example. Use your imagination. What motivates and what deters you? Sign your contract and then have someone that will hold you accountable to sign it as well. Put it somewhere visible as a visual reminder of your commitment to yourself and your goal. If you really want to be creative, have a commitment ceremony with friends and family present.

3–Practice Mindfulness

The world is full of distractions. You walk into your house and see the bag you forgot to take to the charity, the plants that need watering, or the vitamins you neglected to take this morning. We're so distracted that we don't always do the things we should. Mindfulness is a valuable tool that we need to practice every day. Be present. Stay present. Consciously focus your mind on what you are doing at that moment. One excellent way to assist with mindfulness is to do one thing at a time. Don't listen to a podcast while you are getting organized for the day. First, take the bag for charity and put it in the car. Fill up the watering can and water those droopy plants. On your way through the kitchen, stop and think about the benefits of your vitamins, then take them. If you don't do it now, you'll likely move on to other things and forget.

As a side note, I'm a strong believer in the power of the right vitamins for optimal health. Magnesium, for instance, is one of the minerals that many of us are deficient in, and it's great for helping with anxiety and better sleep. If I were truly mindful, I would reflect on the power of my vitamins daily and never forget to take them again.

4–Use the Seinfeld Strategy

Everybody knows Jerry Seinfeld. He's one of the top comedians of all time. According to *Forbes* magazine, he made $267 million in his top year. Ten years later, he was still making a yearly average of about $85 million. (Dipiazza, 2016; see Notes.) The guy is a prolific producer of comedy, movies, and all kinds of content. He's been doing it over and over again.

So how does he do it? He never breaks the chain.

James Clear talks about this in his book, *Atomic Habits*. A young comic once asked Seinfeld, "What advice do you have for a young comic?" He responded, "Write every day. Write some comedy every day." The kid asked, "How do I do that?" "Get a yearly calendar with all the days on one calendar," Seinfeld told him. "Just write every day and cross off a big X on the calendar. Never break the chain of Xs."

Seinfeld's method is useful for something like writing a book, for example, because you can simply focus on writing for a certain amount of time each day. However, this isn't the best strategy for something like doing 200 push-ups or running 10 miles every day. You would get sore and probably pull a muscle. The Seinfeld strategy is about doing something small every day so that you don't break your chain. Try it. You'll feel good about it. It's the small things that add up that make you feel confident—that keep you motivated to do more things and in the end, increase your discipline.

Seinfeld put it powerfully: "Write 15 minutes a day." He didn't say, "Write 10 pages a day." He didn't say, "Write three jokes a day." He just said, "Write every day."

When doing an activity that requires a lot of discipline to complete, like writing, working out, or deep thinking tasks, it's very helpful to start by telling yourself I'm just going to do it for five minutes. It almost always turns into much more time and you end up accomplishing what you needed to do.

This is part of the Seinfeld strategy. If you write every day, some days you'll write for five minutes, but other days you might write for an hour and five minutes. There's no specific amount required to get that X on the calendar. It could be anything, such as deciding not to eat after 6 p.m. or studying a subject to advance your skills just 15 minutes per day. When you achieve that goal, mark that X on the calendar and keep doing it until it becomes a continuous chain. Seinfeld's advice is to never break the chain—and if you do, then just go back to it.

Take Your Mark, LEAD!

Lead Yourself

Each day offers new opportunities to recommit to the discipline needed to accomplish our goals, from fitness to financial freedom, and more. Get your actions to align with your thoughts for greater self-discipline, less procrastination, and ultimately, greater freedom. It's a high-impact process to think about your future self benefiting from your current actions. Once you realize how inextricably linked procrastination and discipline are, you can have more resolve. And remember… *Discipline Developers* find meaningful motivation, defeat procrastination, and take small steps in the direction of their goals to strengthen their discomfort muscle.

Lead Others

Being a *Discipline Developer* as a leader means focusing your team on what matters most. This involves the 80/20 rule, one of the most helpful concepts for life and time management. Also known as the

Pareto Principle, this rule suggests that 20% of your activities should account for 80% of your results. Sometimes this can be hard because the non-producing activities are often more fun to do. Holding your team's focus on what matters takes discipline.

We've all heard the saying, "It's lonely at the top." Sometimes being a leader will require making unpopular decisions. Again, this takes discipline. By using the techniques in this chapter to lead yourself you can make better, sometimes tough decisions to boldly lead others.

To be a champion *Discipline Developer:*

☑ Assume a new identity

☑ Find your why

☑ Start your day with difficulty

☑ Ease into change

☑ Know your strengths and weaknesses

☑ Deeply understand your motivation

☑ Use temptation bundling

☑ Make a commitment contract

☑ Practice mindfulness

☑ Use the Seinfeld strategy

5

PASSIONATE PERSISTER

---

*Passionate Persisters manage their pain and discomfort
using passion, presence, preparedness, positive focus,
and purpose to achieve their goals.*

"Don't give up. Don't ever give up."

**—Jim Valvano, NC State Basketball Coach and
Coach of the 1983 NCAA Division One Champions**

The Cinderella Team

Jim Valvano had a passion for life that made him a natural leader. When I'd walk past his basketball office in the athletic department at NC State University sometimes he'd holler (in his New York accent), "Hey, Kelly P., how's life in the pool?" If I wasn't late for an appointment at the swim office, then I would stop in and chat with Coach V. My several visits with him during the 1983 basketball season were a powerful learning experience for me and one I'll always treasure, especially since his passing.

Coach V was a champion for cancer research, and before he died, he created the *V Foundation for Cancer Research* in conjunction with ESPN. The speech Jim Valvano gave at the ESPY Awards, just less than two months before he died, is a powerful inspiration for never giving up. Of all the champions I've known, Coach V is the perfect one to open this chapter on passionately persisting. He died at age 47, following a nearly year-long battle with metastatic cancer.

Coach V led his team to the 1983 NCAA Basketball Championship against improbable odds, defeating the heavily-favored Houston Cougars, whose amazing team was nicknamed by the press as Phi Slamma Jamma. Houston's players included basketball royalty such as the original twin towers, the 7'-tall Hakeem "The Dream" Olajuwon and 6'7"-tall Clyde "The Glide" Drexler. But with all of Houston's capacity and talent, they lost the national title to a physically smaller, but mentally mightier team, the NC State Wolfpack. In my introduction to this book I asked, "What makes the unlikely person rise to the top of their profession or lead others to victory?" This story is one answer.

Coach V's "survive and advance" strategy was how an unlikely team rose to victory. When I asked Coach V how that strategy worked, he told me, "Kell, it simply means to take things one minute at a time, one hour at a time, one day at a time." **Don't look up at the whole staircase—just climb one step at a time.** Coach V's Wolfpack was nicknamed the Cinderella Team for being so "unlikely" to be at the final of the NCAAs. They were also called the "Cardiac Pack" for almost inducing heart attacks because of their many overtime wins.

Watching the "Cardiac Pack" during March Madness, my senior year at NC State, was definitely a cause for heart palpitations. As they advanced through the tournament, several of their wins happened in overtime, or were double-overtime victories that had me (and all Pack fans) screaming at our TVs. I was also personally invested in the team as I had been an academic tutor for two of the Pack's basketball starters, Dereck Whittenberg and Lorenzo Charles. And Terry "The Cannon" Gannon was a close friend—I even introduced him to his wife, Lisa, one of my college roommates. As much as I wanted them to win for the larger fan base, I wanted to see these champions, *my friends*, achieve the ultimate pinnacle of success in NCAA basketball.

My days as a student-athlete at NC State and the champions I was able to interact with on a day-to-day basis at the athletes-only dining hall, in the athletic department, and beyond, were truly a study in excellence. Winners in this circle also included distance running star Julie Shea, Olympic wrestler Tab Thacker, major league-bound baseball pitchers and brothers, Joe and Dan Plesac, and elite volleyball captains, Martha Sprague and Joan Russo. These champions, along with the legendary Pack swim family, including my closest friends and stud swimmers Amy Lepping and Beth Emery, all inspired me, taught me, and gave me an up-close and personal view of how champions operate. It was at this point in my life when I began a fascination with understanding champions and peak performance.

I'd imagine I can speak for my fellow Wolfpack athletes in saying we were all inspired by Coach V and the 1983 NCAA title of our basketball team. **Surviving and advancing is not just a great strategy for winning an NCAA Basketball Championship, but it is an effective strategy for life.** If there ever was a passionate persister, it would be Coach Jimmy Valvano. In this chapter we are going to look at ways to manage pain and discomfort using passion, presence, preparedness, positive focus, and purpose to achieve your goals.

Survive Suffering

Very different from basketball, endurance athletics is one way to learn about pain and suffering. As a distance swimmer, you're in a different place compared to other athletes. It's you and your thoughts, and when your thoughts become negative, it creates more physical and mental pain. Our mind is highly influential in all realms of life, and you don't have to be an athlete or in an athletic situation to benefit from these mental techniques. Coming up, you'll see how the power of our minds plays a vital role in our persistence. But first, let's meet Leah.

Leah Sees Jesus

Leah Smith is an Olympic champion and distance swimmer who knows about pain. If it were not for Katie Ledecky's domination and legend as the greatest women's distance swimmer in history, Leah Smith would be the name at the top of that conversation. When I met up with her in Las Vegas during the International Swimming League Finals, Leah, who is known for going flat out in her races, told me about how she deals with pain.

"I really haven't had too many races where I wasn't in excruciating pain," Leah admitted. "At the start of a race, I'm like a horse coming out of the gate. My coaches want me to have more of a race strategy and pace myself better, but often I just can't help myself."

"A good example of this was at the 2014 NCAA Championships. I wasn't happy with my swims in the 200 or 500 in the meet leading into the mile. So for the mile, I knew that I had to just lay it all out there. And that's what I did. I went out fast and hard, swimming at the edge of my max effort. I was swimming strong most of the race, then around the 1,200 mark (of 1,650 yards), two girls started to gain on me. I wanted to hold them off, but I was in so much pain."

"That's when the dialogue in my brain started. *I'm dying and I don't know if I can do this. Of course I can do this! Stay in the present moment. I'm okay right now on lap 45, why worry about lap 55? I'm not there yet. I may feel better, or maybe the same. I can handle this moment. Hang in there! I train for this. I did not put in all this time to back off now.* I managed to hold off the girls, but after the race, I remember telling my friends that I had seen Jesus because I'd been in so much pain. But I knew I didn't have to hold onto that much longer," Leah said.

This is a game we can often play in life when we're in a tough situation. *How much longer do I have to hold on?* Leah used the first of the eight tools we're about to unleash for helping us persist through tough times. The beauty of these is that they work in all aspects of life, too.

Eight Ways to Manage Your Pain

This chapter is about enduring, persisting, and, in the words of one of my favorite coaches, Don Easterling, "keep on keeping on." It's not just about persistence in athletics, but also the emotional and mental management of pain, suffering, and challenges thrown our way every day.

1–Stay in the Present

Keeping your thoughts and attention in the present moment is one of the best ways to control suffering. Much of the suffering we endure is based on something we are worried about in the future. Leah's story perfectly illustrates this concept. Additionally, don't worry about the past. It's gone and out of your control. You can't change the past, but you can change the future by how you react in the present moment. Regarding future worries, iconic American novelist and humorist, Mark Twain, said it best. **"My life has been a series of tragedies, none of which actually ever happened."** Don't suffer tragedies needlessly. Pain in the present is key. Don't project that your pain will always be there in the future or think about its meaning. Just deal with it right there. A technique I use with my coaching clients is to verbally complete the phrase, *now I am. Now I am eating. Now I am walking. Now I am doing strength training,* and so on. By completely keeping your focus on the task at hand, and not on the pain, you'll be less likely to engage in worry.

2–Focus on What Feels Good

Find something that isn't tormenting you, focus on that, and be grateful for it. Hone in on what is working. If you are a leader in tough times, what is going right that can bring you some positivity to help you through those tough times? You can do the same for mental or emotional hurts too. Maybe you are having a difficult time with something at work, but everything's going well in your home life. Be grateful for that. This technique is not a permanent fix for problems, but it can certainly help you weather a storm. I love this example that Maria uses in her endurance bike races. She says, "When my legs are burning and exhausted and I don't think I can go another mile, I try to switch my attention to how comfortable my arms are. It gets me through." Try it.

3–Have a Powerful Phrase or Vision

There's a go-to power mantra that helps me whenever I'm feeling stressed. I say to myself: *I am calm. I am peaceful. I am relaxed.* The phrases flow out of me naturally, and they lower my cortisol and blood pressure. What words make you feel better? Be prepared with something positive to help you push forward. It could be singing your favorite song, a series of Oms, or thinking about butterflies, or puppies.

Swimming with Dolphins

Sara Henninger (now Sara Dunn), who was one of my top swimmers when I was coaching at the University of South Carolina, had to sometimes get cortisone shots in her knees. One day I went to the doctor's with her and saw her get two gigantic needle injections, directly into her knee, but she remained so calm. I asked her how she went through the shots without any reaction. She said, "I was not in that room, Coach. I was imagining myself just off a Caribbean island, swimming with dolphins."

Create your happy place. Have something prepared for when something bad comes up. You can change the neural pathway from the worst-case scenario to visiting a Caribbean island, just like Sara did.

4–Be Prepared

One key to perseverance is preparation. Obviously, if you're an athlete, you will have a race or event coming up where you're prepared for pain and suffering. And if you are not, you can still be prepared.

If you're going to the dentist, for example, thinking you're just getting your teeth cleaned, they might find an unexpected cavity, and suddenly you're in pain. Try to have a visualization prepared so you can go somewhere else in your mind for relief.

If you're suffering from a physical ailment, you may not have been prepared going into it. Let's say you pull or strain a muscle, or have sudden back pain. You didn't prepare for that, but by employing some of the techniques in this chapter, you'll be ready to react more positively in multiple scenarios.

Life and leadership can be painful. Suffering can be mental, emotional, or physical. Sometimes when I have to do something difficult as a leader, like fire a subordinate, it's very mentally and emotionally painful for me. But I fall back on the tools in this section, which work for all types of challenges. In the firing example, I might focus on what else is going well on my team and the other people that are high performers and don't have to be let go. Watching out for cognitive distortions is helpful too. If I'm not careful I might jump to the conclusion that this person, whose employment I'm terminating, is going to be on the street, homeless. Instead though, maybe they are miserable in this job and are destined to find their true calling and be fulfilled.

5–Stop Cognitive Distortions

Mental health plays a huge role in one's overall wellbeing, and mental hygiene is the maintenance of one's mental health through proactive behaviors and protocols.

When we are persisting through something challenging, especially if it is long-term and chronic, we can develop deeply ingrained neural pathways that can really bring us down, even causing us to become clinically depressed. This is all based on our thinking, what I call *stinkin' thinkin'*. There is a great technique for simply practicing good mental hygiene or treating real depression, and it is known as Cognitive Behavior Therapy, or CBT.

CBT was researched and created by Dr. Aaron T. Beck, and is based on getting rid of cognitive distortions. When you are trying to passionately persist through challenges, check yourself for as many of these distortions as are applicable. I'd also like to recommend a couple of technological applications for tracking and converting *stinkin' thinkin'* to good thoughts. One is the *Thought Diary* app and the other is called *Woebot*.

If you're not enthused about using technology to help you reshape your thoughts, rest assured, you can always go the old fashioned route. Begin by doing a *thought check*. Ask yourself these four questions, which are the basis of CBT (and of the apps mentioned above), and then journal your answers. 1) What negative thought are you having right now? Identify it against the list of cognitive distortions below, which you can print out and keep in your journal. By doing this you will see just how distorted your thinking might be. 2) How can you challenge this thought? Is it 100% true? 3) What is another way of interpreting the situation? What is a more positive, alternate way to look at it? 4) Finally, *how am I feeling right now?* Generally, you'll find that if you get in the habit of asking yourself these questions at the start of a negative thought, you will feel better and break the cycle of sliding into the abyss of *stinkin' thinkin'*.

Based on Dr. Beck's work, here are the most common types of **distorted thoughts to be aware of**:

Overgeneralization happens when you make a rule after a single event or a series of coincidences. The words "always" or "never" frequently appear in the sentence. This can also be termed *all-or-nothing thinking*.

Mental filters are an opposite to overgeneralization, but with the same negative outcome. Instead of taking one small event and generalizing it inappropriately, the mental filter takes one small event and focuses on it exclusively, filtering out anything else.

Discounting the positive is a cognitive distortion that involves ignoring or invalidating good things that have happened to you.

Jumping to conclusions usually happens in two ways:

Mind reading is when you think someone is going to react in a particular way, or you believe someone is thinking things that they aren't.

Fortune telling is when you predict events will unfold in a particular way, often to avoid trying something difficult.

Magnification is exaggerating the importance of shortcomings and problems while minimizing the importance of desirable qualities.

Emotional reasoning is a way of judging yourself or your circumstances based on your emotions.

"Should" statements are self-defeating ways we talk to ourselves that emphasize unattainable standards. Then, when we fall short of our own ideas, we fail in our own eyes, which can create panic and anxiety.

Labeling is a cognitive distortion that involves making a judgment about yourself or someone else as a person, rather than seeing the behavior as something the person did that doesn't define them as an individual.

Personalization and blame is a cognitive distortion whereby you entirely blame yourself, or someone else, for a situation that in reality involved many factors and was out of your control.

6—Ask for and Give Help

If you have the opportunity to get help, ask for it.

Tough athletes or proud leaders might sometimes feel silly asking for help, but let's not forget that they are human too. Getting help, especially if you're truly suffering from something beyond what you can handle alone, is important.

When I had breast cancer, I used a helpline. If I was fearful and feeling vulnerable, I would call somebody and say, "I'm really worried. This is really scaring me." There's no need to suffer alone, especially not in this world of connectivity with helplines and online support. Then there's the old-fashioned way of just talking with a friend.

One of the other things I did during that time was to create a website called "Swimming Through Breast Cancer." I also went on breast cancer forums to help other people. I thought that when something was bothering me, there was likely somebody going through something even worse. When you're so down and in your own pit, remind yourself that other people are in an even deeper pit. So often, we need to stop navel-gazing and ask, "What can I do to help?"

Is there something that you are suffering through that could become a cause for you to champion? Could you make a difference by improving the world—or at least someone's world? If you can't do it on a large scale, then reaching out to one person can be of significant value as well. One of my favorite quotes attributed to former President Ronald Reagan is, "We can't help everyone, but everyone can help someone." Here's a story about being helped.

Hand-Holding Hell

Going through breast cancer with surgery was an impromptu opportunity to take the best principles and techniques from athletics and apply them in real life.

For those who are squeamish, you might want to skip this story because it is graphic. It's about a very painful experience and one of my scariest situations.

One of the things that most breast cancer patients are required to do just moments prior to a lumpectomy surgery is to receive injections into the nipple of their breast where the tumor is. This is to inject a dye into the area so the surgeon has a visual guide.

After the nurse explained this to me she said, "You can have one person hold your hand because it's going to be hell." I appreciated her honesty and weighed my options. Both my husband and Maria were with me. I looked at Maria, I looked at Mark, and decided, "I want Maria to hold my hand for this." I don't think I hurt Mark's feelings, and Maria says she would've chosen me over her own husband, too. Maybe it was the commonality of us both having breasts, or Maria's motherly, nurturing spirit.

They needed to inject my nipple with four different shots and the needle was huge.

The nurse asked me if I wanted the shots one at a time and to recover in between each, or if I wanted to get all four done as quickly as possible. I don't think it would have mattered either way, frankly, but I chose to get them done as quickly as I could. I've experienced some painful things, but four large needle injections into my nipple are one of the most painful things I'd ever been through.

Yet, as I was lying on that table, looking up at the ceiling, I decided to pull a few valuable tools I had learned as an athlete to mitigate my misery. First, I tried to stay in the present moment and not anticipate the next shot. After the first one I said, okay, I'm okay. Next, I breathed deeply. I also reassured myself with the words *I am calm. I am peaceful. I am relaxed.* Using humor was helpful too. "This is going to feel sooooo good, when it's done." I admit it wasn't that funny, but both Maria and the nurse laughed, and that lightened the mood. Finally, I had asked for help, and there was Maria holding my hand. Sometimes we need someone to hold our hand. We just have to ask.

7–Laugh it Off

One of my future books might be on laughter because it has so much power in helping us get through tough times in life. We've all heard that laughter is the best medicine, but who knew that laughter also helps with persistence? Turns out it does. David Cheng and Lu Wang went so far as to look at the exact role humor has on persistence. Their article, *Examining Energizing Effects of Humor: The Influence of Humor on Persistence Behavior,* found that using humor makes you more persistent. (Cheng & Wang, 2014; see Notes.) And I know this to be true for one of my heroes.

Anyone nicknamed *Trog* has to have a sense of humor. My Dad, known to his grandkids and great-grandkids as *Trog* (short for Troglodyte), is 91 years old. I always appreciate the wisdom of elders, and when I think of my Dad, he's laughing at something and making others laugh. One of his favorite sayings is **"Endure with courage, suffer with dignity, and prevail with a sense of laughter."** I tried to find the credit for that quote online but couldn't, so I asked my Dad where it came from. "I'm not sure," he said, "it's probably a mishmash of things. I've adopted it as my mantra, so when I'm having a bad moment, I say it and it helps me." My Dad has laughed his way through many of life's hardships and he's better for it.

Another quick story about using humor to persist is from a champion you are going to meet again in Chapter 7, the *Peak Performer,* and that's Dan Plesac, the 3X All-Star Major League Baseball pitcher. Whenever Dan would have one of his pitches knocked out of the ballpark in an especially spectacular fashion, after the game, he'd jokingly ask, "Did you see that ball fly out of the park?! Do you think they served meals on that flight?" We must laugh at ourselves. It relieves stress and it just plain feels good!

8—Recognize the Season

A season is a term that is often used in athletics. Think football, baseball, basketball season, and so on. We know that all seasons come to an end. One way athletes get through hard training during "boot camps" and laying a base of grueling workouts is by knowing this intense time will pass. It's only temporary. Well, life works exactly like this too. Bad things that happen to us, tough times, may seem like they will be around forever, but they won't. Life has seasons. Some seasons are bright and sunny, and others are dark and gloomy. And as Winston Churchill said, "If you're going through hell, keep going."

After interviewing many, many champions I've noticed a phrase they often use about hardships they've encountered. They call them "speed bumps," not "stop signs." There will be plenty in life to slow you down—just don't let anything stop you.

Bob Almost Quit Coaching

Bob Bowman, the renowned coach of the greatest swimmer and Olympian of all time, Michael Phelps, almost left the sport of coaching...

Bob and Michael's dynamic partnership earned an unprecedented 28 Olympic medals, 23 of them gold. Bowman was also the head coach of Team USA's men's Olympic team in 2016, and on the Olympic coaching staff in 2004, 2008, and 2012. Since 2015, Coach Bowman has been the head men's and women's swim coach at Arizona State University (ASU).

I interviewed Bob Bowman in late 2019 while he was attending a meet in Greensboro, North Carolina. We talked about his amazing coaching career and how, initially, things hadn't happened as he had wanted. And like many of us, Bob began to wonder if he should quit.

"I was coaching in Napa, California, and I had just taken over as the head coach of the club there. And there was Eric Wunderlich, who was a very good swimmer at the time. He had swum at the University of Michigan and had come out to train with me. There was another good swimmer from Auburn University, Lian Mull. Eric had won the Pan Pacific Swimming Championships in the 100 breaststroke the year before the Atlanta Olympics, and he was the fastest American in that event. Lian had won the World University Games in the 400 individual medley and was third at the Pan American Games, behind Tom Dolan. Needless to say, these guys had a shot at making the Olympic team."

"After about a year with me, they came in and said, 'You know Coach, we love swimming here, we love your coaching, but we just can't train with these little kids anymore.' They were the only two adults in a club full of youngsters, and so they went back to Michigan. I was not in a good place for a long time after that. Eventually, I realized that I had worked really hard at this and had given it everything I've got. But obviously, if it were going to happen, it would have already happened by now. So I decided I was done."

"I thought about going back to school and was looking into maybe becoming a veterinarian for racehorses. So I called David Marsh at Auburn, where they have a good veterinary program. I went down there, met with David, and I was going to become a graduate assistant and coach the distance swimmers. But then Murray Stephens from North Baltimore Aquatic Club offered me a job and asked, 'How much is Auburn going to pay you?' '10,000 bucks,' I said, and Murray offered me $35,000. I told him, 'I'll see you there next week.'"

"So that's how I ended up at the North Baltimore Aquatic Club. That was one of those fortuitous things where I would never have expected it to end up the way it did."

Bob explained the lesson he'd learned from his experience of almost quitting coaching. "I don't want to get too philosophical, but I've done a great deal of reading on this kind of stuff. There's a good book called *The Surrender Experiment* by Mickey Singer, and I highly recommend it. I'm not going to get into a lot of Eastern philosophy, but one of the things they talk about is living in the present moment. Surrender to it instead of always trying to fight things and making something happen. Go with the flow of the way your life is going, and somehow you'll naturally go in the direction that you're supposed to go. I've talked quite a bit to my staff and those I'm close to about surrendering to the universe. What's opening up to you right now? This is where you should go."

When it comes to persistence, there's a dance between sticking it out no matter what and going with the flow. I think I can speak for many people and say we are very grateful that Bob Bowman persisted as a coach.

Winners Quit, Sometimes

Let's talk about quitting. The old saying, "Winners never quit and quitters never win" is simply not true. I'm all for sticking it out when you should, but sometimes it's better to fold and move forward—or in a completely different direction. We need to do this in our personal lives, and we need to do this as leaders. As you've just read, sometimes Bob Bowman believes in surrendering to the universe and going with the flow. When the pandemic shut down almost all swimming facilities for months at a time in 2020, safety was a real concern and competitions were in question. In an unprecedented move, Bob opted to have his Arizona State University swim team sit out, or redshirt as they say, the entire 2020-2021 season. His athletic director supported this, as did many other leaders. But was this considered quitting? No. It was a situation with many moving parts, and one that enduring would not necessarily have best served his team.

Maria and I have had many rich conversations on this topic because she's almost never quit anything in her life, whereas I have quit many, many things, often joking that "winners quit." First I quit ballet, then girl scouts, then various jobs, hobbies, relationships, marriages, business ventures… The list goes on. So I set out to determine if my long-held belief that winners quit was sound, and began my research. I was thrilled when an expert on leadership, and someone I admire, backed up my theory.

So when should you quit? "When it's the wrong thing," said High Performance Coach and *NY Times* best-selling author, Brendon Burchard.

"When I talked with some of the world's highest performers they had an obvious pattern of quitting, and frankly, they quit faster than other people. This is an actual observable pattern. High performers are very conscious of what is right, and most important, what was wrong for them. We all learn that perseverance is crucial, but this doesn't apply when you're doing the wrong thing. We've all held on to things, people, and ideas for too long, so it's a relief to know that quitting is permitted. But here's the takeaway: High performers quit what's wrong, not because they're quitters or they mind the struggle, but because they focus on what matters. They know what their priorities are, and they quit everything else that doesn't fit into those categories," Brendon concluded.

So go ahead and quit things that get in the way of your priorities, your real goals, passions, and purpose. This clears the way for pursuing something you truly love. And you wouldn't quit on that, would you?

This final segment of research could go almost anywhere in this book, because it is a universally valuable approach to mindset— and nearly everything revolves around mindset. This concept explores the differences between a fixed versus a growth mindset.

Researcher and professor Carol Dweck from Stanford University uses the term mindset to describe the way people think about ability and talent. Those people operating from a fixed mindset believe that your abilities are innate and unchangeable. You're born with them. People with a growth mindset, on the other hand, believe that you can improve anything with practice. They relish the process and see failure as an opportunity to learn, develop, and evolve.

Those with a fixed mindset generally focus solely on the results, and view failure as permanent. They take critical feedback as personal attacks and when they fail, they feel foolish. This means that they tend to quit before that can happen. Always make sure you're not quitting because of a fixed mindset.

The good news is you can always transform your mindset from a fixed one to one of growth, by remembering to enjoy the process, and believing that you can improve anything with passion, practice, and perseverance.

Take Your Mark, LEAD!

Lead Yourself

Your toolbox for getting through tough times is now stocked with the eight valuable items we discussed in this chapter. Using these will help you truly realize that the obstacles you face are speed bumps, not stop signs. And remember... *Passionate Persisters* manage their pain and discomfort using passion, presence, preparedness, positive focus, and purpose to achieve their goals.

Lead Others

Leading people to greatness is not for quitters. Leaders with persistence see failure or challenges as a temporary setback, yet no matter what, they keep pushing forward and confronting obstacles, while retaining perspective in stressful situations. Strong leadership requires the trait of persistence. Don't take no for an answer. Some of the best leaders simply demonstrate individual persistence which leads and inspires others, and this characteristic best demonstrates that you first need to lead yourself before you can lead others.

To be a champion *Passionate Persister*:

- ☑ Stay in the present moment
- ☑ Focus on what feels good or what's going well
- ☑ Recall a positive place or phrase
- ☑ Be prepared
- ☑ Stop cognitive distortions
- ☑ Ask for and give help
- ☑ Use humor
- ☑ Recognize the season
- ☑ Quit that thing gets in the way of your priorities, your real goals, passions, or purpose

6

HABIT HACKER

Habit Hackers establish and refine the habits, rituals, and routines that support their physical and mental health and peak performance, and remove those that do not.

"You'll never change your life until you change something you do daily. The secret of your success is found in your daily routines."

—John C. Maxwell, Author and motivational speaker

Jordan Carries His Putter

On March 6th, 2021, I watched professional golfer Jordan Spieth land a hole-in-one at Bay Hill Club and Lodge during the Arnold Palmer Invitational in Orlando, Florida. Spieth aced the par-3, 223-yard second hole. There had not been an ace on this hole in 13 years.

From the tee box, he realized almost immediately that he had sunk the drive. The crowd roared from both ends of the fairway. My husband, a phenomenal golfer himself, almost did a backflip. Spieth high-fived caddie Michael Greller and fist-bumped with competitor Justin Rose.

This was quite a feat, to sink an ace on this particular hole which was ranked as one of the 50 toughest holes on the PGA Tour last season. Spieth landed his ball on the front right edge of the fringe, which kicked left and rolled some 40 feet right into the heart of the hole.

But what happened next is almost as interesting, and an excellent commentary on the habits of champions. As Spieth and his caddie began to walk the 223-yard distance from the tee to the hole to retrieve his ace, Greller handed Spieth his putter. Spieth walked the entire fairway with his putter in his hand. Both he and his caddie were on auto-pilot in preparing to take the next shot. The habit of taking out the putter when approaching the green was ingrained in them both. It wasn't until Spieth got directly in front of the hole that he smiled, realizing he didn't need his putter, and handed it off. This is a simple yet powerful demonstration that when one learns a habit and practices it often, it becomes second nature. It occurs without ever thinking about it.

If I had to pick a trait of champions in business and in life that can bring about success more than any other, perhaps it would be the formation and practice of good habits and routines—and the replacement of bad ones.

Habits vs. Routines vs. Rituals

Before we dive deeper into this chapter, let's discuss the differences between habits, routines, and rituals. Champions use a mix of all three. A habit, once established, is something that you do automatically without much thought, and this includes good, bad, and neutral habits. Things like making your bed, brushing your teeth, deep breathing when you're stressed, smoking, biting your nails, looking at your cell phone too much, or carrying your putter up the fairway as Jordan Spieth did, are all considered habits.

Routines are things we do regularly but require a bit more planning, effort, or brainpower. Routines are not necessarily daily like habits, though they can be. They may also have an element of ceremony to them and could involve another person. Routines include doing exercise or meditating in the morning, going for a walk every evening after dinner, or a pre-game, pre-performance ritual like athletes do prior to competing. In the upcoming *Peak Performer* chapter, I'll walk you through the exact routine we do every week before recording our *Champion's Mojo* podcast.

Now, on to rituals. Rituals can be done daily or as infrequently as yearly, or beyond. What separates rituals from habits and routines is that they carry more meaning and purpose. There's a real emotional connection to our rituals.

If you're a runner, one of your habits could be double-tying your shoelaces. A routine might be doing your stretching exercises three times a week to prevent injury. A ritual could be saving all your race numbers and pinning them onto a bulletin board. In another sport like basketball, a ritual might be cutting down the nets after your team wins the match. Or, as we've all seen on the playing field, winning football and soccer teams ecstatically pour their full cooler of drink on the coach. These aren't habits or routines, they're rituals.

Now that we've clarified *that*, in this chapter we will refer to these three concepts interchangeably. We'll talk about adding and implementing ones to make your life better, and removing any that simply weigh you down.

Change Your Habits, Change Your Life

So far, this book's chapters have built upon the skills that one needs to succeed: first goal setting, then visualizing, then discipline, then persistence. You'll need to call on all of these to bring in the magic of habits and routines.

Want to break a bad habit?

Replace it with a good habit.

However, sometimes it's not so simple. Some habits are not so easy to break; they may border on addiction. I think there's a fine line between things we can be addicted to, that we *don't* necessarily need medical resources for, such as smoking, sugar, and caffeine, and more serious, life-threatening addictions like alcohol and drugs, for which we need outside help. This chapter is going to talk about the less threatening habits we want to change. Let's start with breaking bad ones and then adding good ones.

Breaking a bad habit depends on a few things, such as:

- the amount of time you've had the habit

- if the behavior is fully part of your life

- the emotional, social, or physical rewards one reaps

- how motivated you are to breaking the habit

How Long Will It Take?

In a research article entitled *Making Health Habitual*, habit formation was found to take ten weeks, or about 2.5 months, as a realistic estimate for most people. (Gardner, Lally, & Wardle, 2012; see Notes.)

In the same vein, the evidence-based research outlined in *How are Habits Formed: Modelling Habit Formation in the Real World* suggests that breaking bad habits can take anywhere from 18 to 254 days. (Lally, Potts, Van Jaarsveld, & Wardle, 2010; see Notes.)

This study looked at 96 adults who wanted to change one specific behavior. One person formed a new habit in just 18 days, but the other participants needed more time. It took an average of 66 days for the new behavior to become automatic, according to study results.

In an article entitled *Habit Formation and Change,* the most recent data conducted in 2018 recommends that habit change is most successful when the environment is changed, and while using smartphones and other forms of technology for assistance. (Carden & Wood, 2018; see Notes.) So based on the above research, the old notion that it takes 21 days to make a habit stick may have some validity but, in researching that time frame, I found no scientific basis for it. It appears that it could take anywhere between three weeks and three months to change a habit. But how?

Four Ways to Control Bad Habits

We all have many habits whether we recognize them or not. Making your bed in the morning is a good habit. Looking at your cellphone in the middle of a conversation or in the middle of the night is a bad habit. I'm not here to judge others' habits, but I do want to discuss some of the good and bad habits I've witnessed. We're also going to explore what research says we can do about bad habits, and how to form new ones through the power of routines.

Routines are something champions, business leaders, competent parents, and successful people across the board most definitely use. Habits and routines may not initially sound like game-changers, but they *really* are.

For this chapter, I'd like you, dear reader, to envision one or more habits you would like to break. Then apply some of these techniques and see if they feel like winners to you.

1–Identify the Trigger

The first step in breaking a bad habit is to identify the trigger. What sets off the bad habit? If you drink too much, is the trigger going out with certain friends? If you have a bad habit of looking at your phone too much, is the trigger having it beside you? Do you really need your phone on you all the time? If this is the trigger, can you leave your phone in another room? Is the trigger for biting your nails stress? Then maybe play with a stress ball or silly putty instead. This type of fix ties in with changing your environment.

2–Switch Your Environment and Action

The number one trick for breaking a bad habit is changing your environment. If drinking too much is your bad habit, then don't go to bars. If it's eating too much sugar or eating junk food, remove the temptation. Empty your pantry and refrigerator of all junk food. This changes the environment.

A habit I recently wanted to break was being tied to my emails and feeling like I needed to answer them as soon as they came in. The trigger for me was simply seeing an email arrive in my inbox. To change this environment, now I only look at and answer my emails during a one- to two-hour window in the afternoon, depending on how many messages I have. This allows me not to miss any emails yet limits my email answering environment to designated hours only, instead of an all-consuming 12 hours (sometimes more) each day. Also, now most people I communicate with know that if they miss my afternoon window for answering emails, they will get an answer the next afternoon. I also have the good habit of responding to emails within 24 hours.

Changing my environment from answering emails all throughout the day and usually from my phone (while somewhere random) to a designated time and location of sitting at my desk, has made me so much more productive and free.

And while many of us want to break the bad habit of spending too much time on our smart devices, there can be some value from them in helping with habits. Tracking applications like *Habit You* and *Loop Habit* are highly rated by users for helping them change their behaviors.

3–Let Go of Shame

This is an important one.

Some bad habits are ones that *only you* know that you have, and likely feel ashamed of. These might include bad choices of any kind, but some examples are late-night eating, too much technology, hours of watching worthless entertainment, or constantly hitting the snooze button. They're things we're not proud of.

When we tell ourselves, "Tonight, I will not overeat," and then we do, we can beat ourselves up beyond belief. Our inner voice might say, "Oh, you're so weak. You couldn't even go one day with your goal of not snacking late at night." But we need to let go of shame and say, "It's not easy to break a bad habit, but I can do it. I've overcome other things."

I love the concept of talking with yourself like you would talk to a close friend. If a good friend came to you and said, "I'm trying to break this bad habit and whenever I fail, I just feel like I'm lower than a whale's belly," you would sweetly encourage them and say, "Hey, you can do this. This is something that is not going to be easy, but you can do it." Wouldn't it be nice if we could talk this kindly to ourselves?

Some bad habits are obvious to everyone, and they're out there, out in the open. Others are deep, dark secrets that may not even be as shameful as you think. We're all human. We all have bad things we do to ourselves. Once you shine the light into that dark spot, however, it means you're ready to move forward. But until somebody else knows about it, you're probably not going to make any progress. Let go, share your shame, and unleash positive change.

4–Enlist a Coach or Professional

As an executive coach myself, I would say the number one thing I work on with my clients is habit change. Most coaches of any type are really good at this. If we are taking some of the best of athletics and using that to succeed in life and leadership, then we all need coaches. It's highly doubtful that there's an athlete out there that doesn't have a coach, and if they don't, they are probably not performing at their highest level. Enlisting others' expertise can be a game-changer. There are coaches for everything. If you have a habit that you have tried to change, but can't, try a coach. Coaches don't have to be professional, but they do need to be experts in their fields.

If you think you need medical help or could benefit from professional counseling, then seek a licensed counselor. So, what's the difference between a coach and a counselor? Coaches focus on helping you set and achieve goals, while counselors work with clients on emotional and mental health issues.

In Chapter 1, the *Eager Leader*, we talked about how leaders are learners. This is an obvious habit that many leaders share. But what specific habits do leaders in your industry have that you could ask them to coach you on? We're about to jump into a story from Jack Bauerle. In addition to his anecdote about his unique habit, Jack revealed that when he was a first-year coach he called as many experienced coaches as he knew and got their advice. Now that's a coach enlisting a coach. Who can you enlist to assist you in breaking a bad habit or creating a wonderful one?

Jack Writes a Note Daily

Legendary swim coach Jack Bauerle has been the head men's and women's swim coach at the University of Georgia for 40+ years. Bauerle reached the pinnacle of success when he was selected as the US Olympic head women's swimming coach in 2008. Jack's swimmers have won 31 Olympic medals. He's the second winningest NCAA swim coach of all time and his teams have finished in the top ten at the NCAA championships 50 times.

I talked with Jack about his daily habits and routines when I interviewed him recently. He said that he writes a note of gratitude or encouragement to someone every day. I asked him if that wasn't hard to follow through on, or too much of an effort. He said, "No Kel, once I started doing it, it became second nature to me. Now writing that note just comes automatically to me." Jack also exercises daily, or as he puts it, "I play every day. *Playing* is more important to me than exercising. I like chasing a ball. I like the social aspect of it. I love people."

You could credit part of Jack's success to being a people-person. He values relationships tremendously and takes good care of those relationships. He truly cares about his athletes, and his daily note-writing habit is an extension of his virtue of valuing others. There's no doubt that this daily habit has played a role in the fact that Jack Bauerle is one of the most beloved coaches in all the swimming community.

Use Second Nature's Momentum

The powerful thing about habits is that once they become second nature to you, they require almost no energy. Just like Jordan Spieth carrying his putter down the fairway or Jack Bauerle writing a note every day—there's no decision making, it just gets done.

Making things automatic through habits means they take less energy. If you just do them enough, then they become something that benefits you without having to think about them.

Sometimes just recognizing that we do have good habits already ingrained in us helps us add more, and convert bad ones to good ones. What good habits are you doing right now that you can celebrate?

Rock Routines for Wellness Benefits

In my research for this chapter, I found something that really hit home and made so much sense: Forming new routines actually helps your mental health. (Arlinghaus & Johnston, 2018; see Notes.)

Routines for leaders are important as they can help with controlling pressure, setting boundaries, and creating space to reflect.

As someone who suffered on and off with anxiety, especially before I started doing my CBT, having a routine is truly helpful. Routines can keep anxiety at bay and anchor us. I know that when I don't have a set routine, I can feel like a lost ball in high weeds. Routines reduce stress and pressure. They can help with sleeping and maintaining a healthy diet. They can certainly help with exercise, and all of these things really benefit your mental health and overall wellness.

As humans, we thrive on having a routine. In general, we respond best when we go to sleep and get up at the same time. Our bodies have circadian rhythms, and I believe that routines are more innate and more natural to us than we think. And as I said, I feel out of sorts and un-moored when I don't have a routine. Don't you?

Launch Ideal Days with Morning Routines

Many experts agree that the first five minutes of your day can dictate how the rest of your day goes. Getting into an upbeat emotional state is a great way to start your day. When I wake up, I immediately turn on my cloud-based speaker service (Alexa or Google Home) and crank the volume. Hearing music I love while I make my bed always ignites me and gets me ready for an awesome day. My favorites are *Shiny Happy People* by REM, *Let Your Love Flow* by The Bellamy Brothers, *Happy* by Pharrell Williams, *Lovely Day* by Bill Withers, and *Hallelujah* by Pentatonix. What are your favorite songs to get you going?

Generally, when you wake up your mind can be like the gears on a car, and it is often in the neutral position. If it's raining, your back hurts, or the dog didn't make it out, this can shift you into a negative gear, and then that becomes your attitude for the day. Starting your day on a positive note is incredibly powerful.

I told you that I make my bed every morning. A fun image is thinking about the very first time I ever saw my husband's bedroom when we were first dating. I saw that his bed was neatly made, and I thought, *This is the man for me.* What else would you expect from a former Marine Corps officer? You never know what routine you might share with someone that makes a connection.

I even made my bed before morning swim practices at 4 a.m., back in high school. It's a lifetime habit.

Star-Studded Routines

Oprah Winfrey says that she starts her day with gratitude. The minute she opens her eyes she thinks of what she's grateful for, which makes it an easy thing to do. Many people enjoy keeping a gratitude journal. Another popular morning routine is meditation. A lot of people will meditate first thing, once they get up and get their coffee. They'll do 15, 20, or even just five minutes of meditation. Those are two of the most popular morning routines for leaders.

Exercise is another classic favorite. It's said that Seinfeld meditates, Oprah expresses gratitude, and Tony Robbins jumps into a 57-degree Fahrenheit plunge pool. A cold plunge can be a lot like exercise in that it changes your physical state quickly.

Reap the Rewards of Movement

If there's one habit or routine I think everyone should add to be a happier, healthier leader and person, it's exercise. One of my most passionate missions is to encourage people to move their bodies. In some seasons of your life, you'll be able to exercise more than others. There have been times in my life where I exercised every single day, or as often as I possibly could. There have also been times when I have gone weeks without exercising.

Exercise can offer something for everyone. Know that if exercise is something you dread, it's something you won't maintain. Be creative. Instead of using the word exercise, let's just call it movement then. Let yourself off the hook and do something fun and easy. Go on a walk if you can. Some people can push themselves and enjoy vigorous activity without feeling like it's a brutal task, and then there are people who don't like exercise because they think it has to be punishingly vigorous. It doesn't.

Take a gentle walk, play frisbee, or ride a recumbent bike at the gym while watching a movie. Make it fun. It's all about your mindset. I'm finding I've now notched down my competitiveness. I went for a run the other day, only two miles, and I held 13-minute miles. That's *double* my former pace, at a *third* of my former distance, but you know what? It was all I could do. So that's what I did.

Exercise does not have to be grueling. It doesn't have to be something you hate. Find something you love and do it. If it's watching a movie while you ride an exercise bike, then do that. Exercise is not a bad word, but if you think it is, then just say *it is my daily time to move my body!*

Sleep Better with Healthy Habits

Sleep is vital; it is the thing that drives healthiness. A lack of quality sleep breeds disease. If you get solid sleep, it can speed healing, make you smarter, and make you healthy. I think evening routines can help lead you into a good night's sleep.

Regulating the good and bad of light exposure from the sun and your computer and/or phone is of the utmost importance for sound sleep and overall wellbeing. Neuroscientist Andrew Huberman says we need light from the sun when we first wake up, just a few minutes each day, to regulate our circadian rhythms. He says that our eyes respond to the different yellow, orange, and golden hues of the morning sun to wake us up and make us feel good. And then in the evening, there are different hues from the setting sun that start kicking off melatonin-inducing sleep. **Dr. Huberman says that inversely, if we have light in our eyes from our phone or computer screens between 11 p.m. and 4 a.m., this kicks off a pro-depressive circuit in our brains.** That's a big statement, meaning that looking at your cell phone in the middle of the night might cause depression. It's also important to turn off computers and phones 30–60 minutes before bedtime, again for light regulation and not disrupting circadian rhythms. (Huberman & Rivera, 2020; see Notes.)

Experts also say that for the best sleep, one should have the room really dark, at about 69F degrees. (Mizuno & Okamoto-Mizuno, 2012; see Notes.) And if you still have trouble falling asleep, I recommend

Kathryn Nicolai's comforting book entitled, *Nothing Really Happens: Cozy and Calming Stories to Soothe Your Mind and Help You Sleep.*

Form New Routines

A new thing I've made part of my educational routine is listening to uplifting podcasts. Podcasts are great for bundling work tasks. My favorite kinds are inspirational, educational, and sports podcasts. Additionally, now that so many books are available as audiobooks, it makes it easy to keep up on my wish list of books I'd like to consume.

I like to listen when I'm folding laundry, emptying the dishwasher, or doing something where my hands are busy, but my mind is free. If I'm doing menial tasks, listening to something positive helps improve the moment. What new routines can you add to your life for efficiency or simply joy?

Balance Routines within Your Lifestyle

However, for anyone feeling the pressure of, "Oh my gosh, I have too many routines," it is okay to let some go. Routines are there to help get you to do things that can become automatic, like exercise or quitting smoking, but you can give yourself a break. Listen to your own needs. Have some routines, but don't go crazy. Don't take routines to the extreme so that they feel like a prison. And while you hopefully don't have too much pressure in your life, routines can help if you do.

Ten Minutes while Michael Stretched

When I asked Bob Bowman how he got through the pressure of the 2008 Beijing Olympic Games, he credits preparation, presence, and a helpful routine. "In Beijing," he says, "I was much more experienced at the whole process, which helped me with my stress. Michael [Phelps] and I had it completely mapped out and we'd been rehearsing it beforehand. We knew the timing between the events we had done, the triples we did. So there was a whole list of things that we were focused on. We were much more automated, so I didn't have to worry about things as much." Bob explains that every morning, he would take ten minutes while Michael was stretching to go into the pool, look around, and try to drink everything in with his senses. "There was so much that I wanted to remember, and even today I actually remember everything about it. It's crazy when you consciously do that. That small morning routine actually had a calming effect on me. I was like, *Wow, this is super cool. Not many people are ever going to be in this position. We're here. Things are going okay. Everything's going to go well today.* We were really trying to take it moment by moment and not think ahead or look back on what we'd done."

Bob also explained the importance of his daily routine, which included some time in the gym, alternating between weights and cardio. "I try to do that at all meets because it really helps. Working out just keeps me from sitting around and letting my mind go crazy about things. Other than that, I tried to get to know a lot of great people on that team. Mark Schubert has been a good mentor for me, and in many ways he helped us get through it. Frank Busch and Jack Bauerle, my great friends, were there too. So it's fun to just hang out with them and keep things light. Eddie Reese was the head men's coach, so I relied on him to help me de-stress too."

Nowadays, Bob's routine involves getting up every day at the same time. "I'm an early riser on most days, so I'm up at about 4:45 a.m. I usually wake up before the alarm because my body's on a schedule. I go to bed at about 8:30 p.m. It's a solid routine that makes me feel good." Obviously a champion leader like Bob Bowman knows the value of habits and routines.

Take Your Mark, LEAD!

Lead Yourself

Start by writing out which habits you would like to remove and those you would like to add to your life. Then review the checklist below for transforming yourself into a champion *Habit Hacker*. And remember... *Habit Hackers* establish and refine the habits, rituals, and routines that support their physical and mental health and peak performance, and remove those that do not.

Lead Others

There is no doubt that effective leaders often have valuable habits, routines, and rituals. This is one skill that powerfully carries over from leading yourself to leading a work team or family. If you've mastered habits in your own life then you can certainly master them as a leader. According to Entrepreneur.com, there are eight habits of highly successful leaders:

- They read every day

- They focus on challenging tasks

- They make their health a priority

- They learn from people they admire

- They plan the next day the night before

- They keep their goals in front of them

- They take action even when it is scary

- They have a powerful, inspiring "why"

To be a champion *Habit Hacker:*

Quit the bad ones.

☑ Be patient with yourself because habit-changing takes time

☑ Identify your trigger for bad habits

☑ Switch the environment and action and replace them with better choices

☑ Let go of all shame

☑ Enlist a coach or a friend

Start the good ones.

☑ Use momentum

☑ Visualize the benefits and set up and reap rewards

☑ Balance new, better habits with your lifestyle so they are authentic and don't overwhelm you

7

PEAK PERFORMER

Peak Performers combat performance anxiety and perform at their best through preparation, routine, and a focus on their own individual mindset.

"Pressure is a privilege—
it only comes to those who earn it."

—Billie Jean King, Former World #1 tennis professional

Ryan Takes the Middle Ground

Ryan Murphy had just turned 21 years old when he took on some of the most powerful pressure one can experience, the Olympic Games. He is definitely a peak performer. At the 2016 Summer Olympics, Murphy swept the backstroke events by winning gold in the 100- and 200-meter backstroke and the 4×100-meter medley relay. His leadoff, backstroke portion of that relay broke the world record. When I talked with Ryan, he told me that he handles pressure by practicing staying balanced and not letting himself get too high or too low. This is a strategy he employs in all his less important meets leading up to big performances. If a meet is low-key, for example, he tries to visualize it as pressure-filled so he can practice being in that mental space. And if he's in a real pressure situation, he tries to soften the pressure by pretending he's in a low-key situation. He doesn't like to get too high or too low.

Ryan also believes that the more you expose yourself to pressure-filled situations, the better you become at handling them.

Peek at Peak Performers

The term *Peak Performer* can conjure up many different images of those at the top of their game, like an Olympic athlete, a concert pianist, or an attorney arguing her case in the courtroom. It also applies to competent, confident leaders. Whichever you see when you hear this term, chances are these gamers all have much in common. First, they can't be too anxious to perform.

Axe Performance Anxiety

One cannot be a *Peak Performer* if they can't control their pre-event jitters. Like Ryan Murphy in an Olympic final, coming in as a relief pitcher in the major leagues can feel like being in a pressure cooker. In this chapter, you'll meet mental-toughness guru, Dan Plesac, and we're going to break down some of the basic principles and top tricks from the best in the business. Let's hear from Dan now.

Dan Inscribes His Baseball Glove

Dan Plesac knows about peak performance. He's a record-holding Major League baseball player and 3X All-Star. He played 18 seasons as a Major League pitcher, spending time with six different teams, including the Milwaukee Brewers. In all that time, he was never on the disabled list and never had surgery. He is the leader for the Brewers in appearances, saves, and earned-run average, playing in 1,064 games total in his career. Those statistics require some serious mental toughness.

I've had the honor of knowing Dan for a long time and see him as a mentor. Dan and I met as athletes at NC State University and have remained friends for decades. I interviewed him for the *Champion's Mojo* podcast and we named that episode "Mental Toughness, Extra Effort."

During Dan's baseball career he permanently inked MTXE (for Mental Toughness, Extra Effort) on his baseball glove and on the inside of his cap as a visual reminder. He says, "For those 18 years I pitched in the big leagues, I used MTXE. The mental game is everything."

White Ball, Brown Glove

Dan says, "I think it's so important to have a plan. A mental coach with the Milwaukee Brewers taught me that you should try to get into that zone where everything is really quiet. Michael Jordan used to talk about being in that space. You should only be concerned about what you're doing. This is true at any level, whether it's sports or business. When you're operating at that optimum level, you're not hearing the outside noise. And that's the toughest part about being a baseball player or a swimmer or a runner—not paying attention to everyone around you, or the person in the lane next to you. For me, the battle was getting that white ball into that brown glove as many times consistently."

During our interview, Dan told me what he would do or say to himself in the heat of battle, whether professionally or as an athlete. "As crazy as it sounds, each time before I came into a game from the bullpen, I would throw my last warm-up pitch. Then, as the ball was being thrown down to second base, I would stop my jog out to the mound, bend down, untie my shoestring, and tie it up again. That was my cue, my trigger to myself to slow everything down. At that moment, I'd simplify what I needed to do by just telling myself, *Put the white ball into the brown glove.*"

Dan continues. "My untying and tying of my shoe was my mental way of telling myself, *Okay, slow down. Focus on what you need to do. Get that white ball to the brown glove. Don't pay any attention to the fact that it's a household name standing there in front of you. Don't pay attention that it's Don Mattingly, Cal Ripken, or Dave Winfield.* I grew up watching those guys on television as a kid, so they could have been intimidating—but I didn't allow them to be."

The key takeaway here is to use (or develop your own) simple cues like MTXE and "White ball, brown glove," to remind yourself of your mental and physical preparation and help you stay *in the zone* during key performance moments.

Eight Tenets for Better Performance

One thing every champion has experienced is the expectation that comes with performing at a high level. Whenever there is an expectation to perform at your best, there is an opportunity to experience performance anxiety.

When you're feeling pressure, tell yourself what a privilege it is to be at a level where your performance will be judged. **Looking at pressure as a privilege lets some air out of that balloon.**

Let's look at eight techniques that can help you perform better and deal with pre-performance anxiety.

1–Depend on Preparation

Prepare as if your performance depends on it, because it does. **Whenever you feel anxious going into something, you can reduce the anxiety by simply being ready.** Anxiety certainly goes up when you're not prepared, but the truth is that you can prepare well and still be anxious. Preparation can look different for different endeavors, but the commonalities of ample practice, strong technique, visualization, and a strong mindset are always there. If you are well prepared and still feeling anxious, there are seven more points to help you.

2–Rely on Routines

If you recall in the last chapter, Bob Bowman's routines helped him keep pressure away while he coached Michael Phelps to a historic performance. Next is an example of how you can use routines in another scenario.

Podcast Pump-Up

Recording and hosting a podcast is a performance. Through hard work and a lot of what is in this book, our *Champion's Mojo* team has created a highly popular, award-winning show in an extremely competitive, cutting-edge industry. More than two years old and with over 100 published episodes, our podcast is well established in the burgeoning world of podcasting. We were thrilled when we recently got the attention of the CG Sports Network, who approached us to partner with them, which we accepted. This raised the stakes even higher, as now we not only want to be great for our listeners but for our new network's CEO and Sports Agent, Cejih Yung. Because I have a high expectation of our performance during each podcast, I usually am a little nervous each time we record an episode. Our preparation routine helps me get through the stage fright and perform at my best.

Here's what we do. We call it our *podcast pump-up*. Right before each recording, Maria and I always set an intention, out loud, that we're going to do a show that will inspire, motivate, and inform our listeners. We also ask that the words come easily and wisely to us and our guests. Then we throw our arms in the air, like a V for victory, put a smile on our faces and shout, "Yay!" This brings energy into our bodies and gets us pumped! We have our guests do it with us too. Since our guests are always champions, they get it and are happy to join in. We do this before every single show. This is the routine that helped us get and stay on top.

If you want to perform better, at almost anything, simply focus on having a routine that serves to achieve your desired outcome. Set your intentions, and think about what you have to do to put in a great performance. Where would you like to perform better? Could you add a routine to enhance that? Are you a leader who runs meetings, a salesperson prepping to make cold calls, a Mom about to have a difficult talk with a child? Pump-ups work in all these cases. Champions have routines.

3–Visualize Victory

Visualization can enhance performance and combat anxiety. We've gone over this skill in-depth in Chapter 3, the *Vibrant Visionary*, and now is the time to put that to work for you in seizing your victory. You've learned about how driven we are to have a great podcast. I visualize the data checker on my computer and imagine the large number of people that have downloaded our show. I visualize these successes with all my senses—sight, smell, and sound. Remember that because of the reticular activator, the mind cannot tell the difference between something that you've done and something you've visualized repeatedly. If you have a performance coming up and you visualize it enough, it becomes very real in your mind, and then in reality. If you've already visualized a successful performance, then that should minimize your nervousness as well.

4–Let Music Be Your Muse

Listening to music is also another way to calm performance anxiety and enhance your showing. Depending on whether you need to calm yourself down or pump yourself up, picking the right type of music is key. Think of all the Olympians you see wearing headphones before they compete. You can use music before anything you may be nervous about doing. Music has the power to change your mental and emotional state for the better.

5–Stay in Your Lane

Dan Plesac's narrative reinforces that another effective way to deal with performance anxiety is to focus on the process, not the outcome. He also says not to worry about what others are doing, only what you are doing.

At the end of the day, the only thing you can control is what you're doing in your own space and world. Don't try to think about what the person next to you is doing. You can't control your competitors or the conditions around you. The most important thing is to show up and do what you can do, which happens in your lane and no one else's.

6–Feed off Anxiety

Interpret anxiety as rocket fuel. **Adrenaline gives you super strength,** and this may be my favorite technique whenever I have performance anxiety. Contrary to popular perception, performance anxiety can be a great way to boost your performance.

Think of it this way: Imagine you have some big performance coming up. Maybe you're about to start an important race or business meeting. If you aren't filled with adrenaline and some anxiety, then you're not going to perform as well as you possibly could. The way I see it, anxiety can act as a free battery charge.

What you need to understand is that it's possible to get something positive out of all that anxiety. Anxiety triggers the production of hormones such as endorphins, adrenaline, and cortisol that can fuel you to perform better.

Sometimes it helps to have butterflies in your stomach. Anxiety can be a fuel—not an obstacle—to your successful performance.

People who put themselves out there by investing money, time, emotion, and other people's resources in their performance are the most courageous. Think about people who try out for the Olympics. They say, "I'm going to try to make the Olympic team," then they build a team around them—coaches, trainers, family members, friends, doctors, massage therapists, and other specialists. All these people commit to supporting them as an Olympic hopeful and are invested in the outcome. These hopefuls put it all on the line, and this pressure can cause intense anxiety. It takes a lot of courage and skill to deal with expectation.

Here's the story you might be telling yourself if that big expectation doesn't come to fruition. *If I fail, then I'm going to be embarrassed. I'm going to look bad. I'm going to let my team down, and others might think I'm a loser.* All this negative self-talk and pressure bring about anxiety, some of which you can use and some of which you need to mitigate. Never use negative self-talk to bring about anxiety. Feed off the anxiety that happens organically.

7–Ask, So what? What if?

In his book, *The Nuts and Bolts of Psychology for Swimmers,* Dr. Keith Bell explains how to deal with performance anxiety. Recently I saw him at a swim meet, and I told him how his book greatly helped my swimming career when I read it as a young swimmer.

One of my favorite things from the book was adding a "So" to your "What ifs." Let's say you're anxiously thinking, "What if I invest time, money, and other people's resources into this and still fail?"

The solution is to ask, "So? So what? So what if I fail?" I've realized that even if I do fail, I'm still okay and, in fact, I'm better for the journey. Let's say you ask someone out and they say no. So what? There are a million fish in the sea. You flub your speech at your office meeting. So what? Go for that promotion and don't get it. So what? Maybe that wasn't the best job for you and you'll be transferred to do something that you're better at. This is the mental space you have to be in to conquer performance anxiety.

8–Follow in Footsteps

One sure-fire way to perform better is to emulate someone who is already performing at a level you would like to hit. Watch what winners do. Find a role model and learn their secrets. Study them. Ask them for help. This next story is a wonderful illustration of being taken under someone's wing.

Mary T. and Mel: Butterflies of Gold

We can't talk about peak performers without mentioning one of the greatest swimming performers of all time, Mary T. Meagher. What Meagher did has stood the test of time, as one of the greatest Olympic Champions ever. She broke the mold in how fast one can swim butterfly. She broke the world record five times in the 200-meter butterfly, held it for 21 years, and 35 years after her top swim performances, her world-record time would have made all US Olympic Teams including 2008, 2012, and 2016. She's known as Madam Butterfly. But how did she deal with pressure?

In talking with Mary T. she said, "I didn't feel pressure early on. I was pretty naive. I feel like my success was something that just kind of happened to me. My coach sat me down when I was 14 and said, *Hey, there's this meet next year called the Olympics. That's our next goal.* Okay, so maybe I'm exaggerating a bit, but honestly, I don't think I'm that far off in remembering our conversation. The Olympics were not a goal of mine from a young age, so when the 1980 boycott happened I wasn't as devastated. I thought, *Maybe I'll go back to high school and play some field hockey.*" From her first world record at 14, Mary T. went on to swim in the 1984 and 1988 Olympics, winning five Olympic medals. She was a role model for just how fast someone can swim butterfly.

Enter Mel Stewart, 1992 Olympic Champion in the 200-meter butterfly. He swam his first Olympics in 1988 on the same team as Mary T. Stewart credits Mary T. for helping him become a champion and says she was a real role model. "Mary T. really took me under her wing and was kind and supportive. She played a big role in helping me become an Olympic champion. She told me that the secret to swimming butterfly is to become as comfortable doing butterfly as I was doing freestyle." **When we are curious and watch what winners are doing, it can expedite our own success.**

Hit Peaks by Knowing Your Strengths

What if you could take a test that would tell you your most powerful strengths? You can! Research shows that if you have an awareness of your character strengths, you are nine times more likely to flourish. Christopher Peterson and Martin Seligman, well-known researchers in the field of positive psychology, are the gurus and founders of this research. (Peterson & Seligman, 2007; see Notes.)

As found on PositivePsychology.com, being cognizant of your character strengths can help you to have positive emotions, engage with others effectively, have meaning in life, and achieve goals. **Boosting your strengths is way more effective than focusing on correcting deficits.** The science of character strengths is part of the positive psychology movement.

The positive psychology movement is more than 25 years old and was born as a reaction to the focus on mental illness, bad behavior, and negative thinking in psychology. Thousands of studies have confirmed that finding and reflecting on our strengths can help us offset negative experiences, and manage problems more effectively. And with the increase in depression since the pandemic, this is a helpful tool in boosting mood.

There are a lot of excellent materials available to help you discover your own individual strengths, but the very best place to start is at viacharacter.org. This website has a quiz that will tell you your character strengths for free. VIA stands for "Values in Action Inventory," and questions are based on your values and virtues. After you take this survey, you will receive a list of your 24 character strengths ranked in order. Your top five are known as your signature strengths.

By focusing on using your signature strengths you will have greater insight into giving power and purpose to your goals. I've had increased success in using this tool with my coaching clients—this really can be a game-changer.

Deal with Depression and Anxiety

First, if you or someone you know are having thoughts of suicide, please contact the Suicide Prevention Lifeline at 800-273-8255 in the US, or seek out help in your local area.

In leading our best lives and hitting our peak performance, we must keep depression and anxiety under control. Top performers and champions are not immune to these challenging mood disorders. Next up you'll find the *Depression and Anxiety Toolkit*, a list of useful steps to help combat these negative mental states. This toolkit contains eight in-depth steps along with four bonus steps for helping those with mood disorders. **There is also a much more comprehensive and interactive version of this list on our website at ChampionsMojo.com/toolkit.**

So if you, or someone you know, needs tools to tackle negative mental states, here's a good place to start.

1-Exercise! Everyone who wants to heal from depression and anxiety should use exercise to improve their mental health. It's been proven that, in some cases, exercise can be as effective as drug treatments for depression. (Harvard Health Publishing, 2013; see Notes.)

2-Get hopeful and inspired by watching Stanford psychiatrist Dr. David Burns' 18-minute TEDx Talk called *Feeling Good*, which explains Cognitive Behavior Therapy (CBT) and its effectiveness.

3-Read or listen to Dr. David Burns' book entitled ***Feeling Great: The Revolutionary New Treatment for Depression and Anxiety.*** It's available in print and audio format, and can be found anywhere books are sold. For me, this book was the catalyst in quickly turning around any depressive or anxious episode I entered.

4-Download the CBT *Thought Diary* or *Woebot* app. If you're not into apps, you can simply journal your thoughts as you work through Dr. Burns' book. Use the app or practice daily journaling to change your thought patterns. Check back to Chapter 5, the *Passionate Persister*, where we list the ten cognitive distortions and how to do a *thought check* without an app.

5-Regulate the good and bad of light exposure from the sun and your electronic devices. In Chapter 6, the *Habit Hacker,* we learned from neuroscientist Andrew Huberman that we need light from the sun just a few minutes a day to regulate our circadian rhythms and make us feel good. Inversely, if we have light in our eyes from screens between 11 p.m. and 4 a.m., this kicks off a pro-depressive circuit in our brains.

6-Start a media fast. Try to avoid the news for 30 days and I bet you will notice an improvement in your feeling of wellbeing. I learned in journalism class that "if it bleeds, it leads." Drama sells, and mainstream media is not putting out content to inspire us. They want to shock us into reading their headlines, and sadly negativity grabs our attention more than positivity does. Replace the news with uplifting movies, podcasts, audiobooks, and music. And remember that social media is not a real friend either! Search YouTube for social media expert Bailey Parnell, who explains how limiting social media decreases loneliness and depression. Do this for your mental health.

7-Meditate or pray just ten minutes a day. A Harvard study entitled *How Meditation Can Help with Depression and Better Manage*

Stress and Anxiety, is part of the mountains of evidence on how meditation improves our mental and physical wellbeing. (Harvard Health Publishing, 2018; see Notes.) Prayer is also proven to lower stress and, some say, may even produce miracles. Check out TheHealing-Mind.org with Dr. Martin Rossman, where you will find helpful resources, including a free *Positive Worry Meditation*. Begin with just ten minutes of quiet, then reflect on how much better you feel.

8-Journal daily gratitude. Use your CBT *Thought Diary* app, a simple notebook, or gratitude jar, and list three things each day for which you are grateful. The power of gratitude is priceless. And if you are not convinced, there's a comprehensive article on PositiveP-sychology.com that lists the 80+ benefits of journaling. (Ackerman, 2021; see Notes.)

Four Extra Tools for Wellbeing

1-Supplement a good diet with vitamin D, omega-3 fatty acids, and magnesium. All three have been proven to help with depression. And as mentioned in Chapter 6, the *Habit Hacker*, magnesium also improves sleep and lessens anxiety.

2-Help someone else. This gives us purpose, which makes us feel more optimistic, connected, and valuable.

3-Be loving and kind to yourself. Treat yourself as someone you dearly love. Picture yourself as a toddler. Try putting a baby photo of yourself on your phone screen.

4-Simplify and unclutter your life and your physical environment. Give away stuff you don't need. Cut ties with negative people.

MEDICAL DISCLAIMER: *The Depression and Anxiety Toolkit* is not intended to be a substitute for professional medical advice, diagnosis, or treatment. Always seek the advice of your physician or other qualified health providers regarding any medical condition.

If you are experiencing depression, there are medications that many people find effective for these conditions—but the steps referenced in the *Depression and Anxiety Toolkit* focus solely on non-pharmacological tools.

Keep Showing Up

Besides all the other concepts, a simple piece of wisdom that will assist you in becoming a *Peak Performer* is to keep showing up—whether that means showing up for yourself, for someone else, or for that dreaded 5 a.m. practice. Be open and willing to show up to continually learning how to become a better leader, or how to run your business more efficiently. This advice could also be in the *Passionate Persister* chapter, but I've placed it here because, in reaching the top of your game, there is a tremendous benefit to showing up day after day, week after week. It takes time, patience, and courage to reach the summit. How many times do we hear about a person who is an "overnight success," when, in reality, they have been working at their craft for years, if not decades? Continually show up and good things will happen.

Take Your Mark, LEAD!

Lead Yourself

One of the greatest hindrances to peak performance is the anxiety we can experience prior. If you can control that, you can soar! Use the checklist below to become a champion *Peak Performer.* And remember… *Peak Performers* combat performance anxiety and perform at their best through preparation, routine, and a focus on their own individual mindset.

Lead Others

Walk through this chapter with your work team and family to help lead them to the best ways to reach their peak and understand performance anxiety. And why not have each of your group members take the VIA Character Strengths quiz at viacharacter.org? As a leader, you'll have a much better overview of what strengths each person possesses, and it will open your eyes to the diversity of talent within your team. When my *Champion's Mojo* co-host Maria and I took the quiz, we did not share one common top-five strength. This made us feel like we were a diverse and more effective duo because each of us brought something different to the table.

To be a champion *Peak Performer:*

☑ Prepare like your performance depends on it

☑ Rely on routines

☑ Visualize victory

☑ Let music be your muse

☑ Stay in your lane

☑ Feed off anxiety

☑ Ask yourself, *So what? What if...?*

☑ Follow in a winner's footsteps

☑ Know and use your strengths

☑ Keep showing up

8

CONFIDENCE CARRIER

Confidence Carriers use and develop a strong inner voice to power a can-do mindset.

"I do think that you can develop confidence over time. You can put things in your back pocket that are going to build confidence, things that you can reference."

—Greg Meehan, 2021 Head US Olympic and Stanford University Women's Swim Coach

No-Show at Pfizer

I sat in a large auditorium-style conference room in Reston, Virginia, with hundreds of other Pfizer pharmaceutical sales representatives, looking at an empty stage.

It was a placid sea of black, navy, and gray business suits worn by both men and women, who, for the most part, had pleasant symmetrical faces and trim bodies. We'd been instructed to wait quietly in our seats for the next item on the meeting agenda: a motivational speaker who was going to come out and pump us up. I'm sure our bosses were anticipating that the hired speaker, an Olympic gold medalist in archery, was going to motivate us to raise our sales numbers and hit our targets, pun intended.

This was one of my favorite events as a member of the Pfizer sales force. It was called a Plan of Action meeting, a POA, and it was usually held in a geographical district with only about a dozen or so members of your district team present. On this occasion, however, the region's entire division of one of Pfizer's primary care sales forces was there. The room was full, with every seat taken. At the front, there was a large, professionally designed, raised stage set up with outstanding quality sound, lights, and decor for maximum message delivery.

The wait for the speaker to come on stage continued, and I thought this lull was a good time to take a bathroom break so that my well-hydrated body wouldn't make me miss a minute of the upcoming talk. As I left the auditorium and headed down the hall, I passed a scrum of district and regional managers with their heads together having, what looked like, a rather serious discussion. On my way back from the bathroom, my own district manager, who was just leaving the circle, greeted me. I smiled and asked her what was causing the wait.

She told me that the Olympian who was scheduled to talk had a three-hour flight delay and was not going to make it to speak to the group. I was initially disappointed. Then my inner voice said, *I could speak to this group about peak performance and motivate them to hit their targets...* I had spoken to many large groups before. Once, as the Head Women's Swim Coach at USC, I had spoken to 10,000 Gamecock fans at a pep rally. And of course, as a swim coach I had motivated plenty of my own teams.

But wait. Was I, a regular entry-level sales rep, about to volunteer to speak to a room full of Pfizer pharmaceutical sales representatives, hospital reps, district and regional managers—most outranking me? Was I going to offer to get up on a big stage on the spot and give an inspiring speech? Was I going to put it all on the line? What was I thinking?! I needed to call up some confidence.

When you are hired by Pfizer, they tell you that statistically, it is harder to be hired by their company than to be admitted to Harvard University. I've never seen the official stats on that, but even if that is just Pfizer lore, it is a bit daunting to think of the high caliber of people in the audience that day. I do know that my peers in Pfizer were former military officers, top sales performers from many other industries, and certainly several with impressive medical backgrounds, all unlike my own. I had come to Pfizer after being a Division One Head Swim Coach and then taking time off to help my oldest brother, who had three children under the age of eight and whose wife had recently suddenly passed away.

Flashback four years before this POA meeting to my first week of training with Pfizer in New Jersey, when our training class was treated to a big reception to introduce us to Pfizer's upper management. At that time, the highest position in the Pfizer sales force was the Vice President of Sales. The VP of Sales was usually an older man with decades of experience in Pfizer, and often one who had held a military leadership position.

All of us new trainees went through a reception line to meet our new VP of Sales, who fit the above description to a tee. He asked each of us what position we had held before being hired by Pfizer. I remember I smiled and proudly told him that I had been a D1 Head Swim Coach. Well, the smile was quickly knocked off my face when he sternly replied, "That's a stretch! I sure hope you can hack it."

Now, flash forward again to the missing Olympian speaker. Should I offer to speak in his place? I just needed to recall that interaction with my VP of Sales to say to myself, *Yes, of course I can hack it! I've got this!* I brought in my can-do attitude and recalled that in my second year with Pfizer I had finished as the number one or number two performer in sales in my entire division on my top three products, Zithromax, Zoloft, and Zyrtec. This had earned me what, at that time, was purported to be one of the largest bonuses in Pfizer sales history. I used my history of success to build up my confidence.

Stepping in for an Olympian

In the hallway, on the way back from the bathroom, I said to my district manager, "I want to help. I'd like to volunteer to speak to this group and pump them up for peak performance." I knew that if I was disappointed that we weren't going to have a speaker, then others would feel the same way. I had many athletic stories that were motivating. I wanted to see if I could step up, help out a situation in need, and test myself. I was scared of the risk but knew the risk might be worth it.

After my district manager consulted with Bob Brinker, the Eastern Regional Training Director and organizer of the entire event, he gave me the nod. My DM came back and said, "Kelly, you're on stage in five minutes, I know you can do this! I believe in you! And by the way, we need you to speak for 20 minutes."

There's something about doing an activity that really scares you, but that you feel you are competent to do, that builds your confidence muscle like nothing else—once it's done. And let me tell you, I was really scared.

So just five minutes after I had officially volunteered to replace the guest speaker, I was on stage facing hundreds of my peers and upper management, sharing my ideas and stories from being an athlete myself and coaching champions. I spoke for 20 minutes and yet it seemed like five. I was in flow, or *in the zone* as some call it. What I could never have imagined was that the audience would give me a rousing round of applause.

I would later come to find out that stepping in to replace that missing speaker was the best thing I could possibly have done for my career—not to mention all the invaluable self-confidence it gave me! Little did I know that on that day I had sown seeds that would bear real fruit down the road.

Fast forward a few years, to the creation of a new job position that was *the* job of my dreams within Pfizer. The position was for Regional

Training Manager for the Mid-Atlantic Region, and was based in Reston, VA. The job description was to train sales representatives in large groups on peak performance, leadership, accountability, emotional intelligence and more—Pfizer's version of an internal corporate trainer. This was perfect for me. While I liked being a sales rep, calling on doctors and detailing them on Pfizer's products, I was somewhat obsessed with this newly posted position because it used all my skills from my coaching days and encompassed my passion for personal development—my own and helping others with theirs.

Besides the obvious compatibility for the actual duties of the position, if I were to get the job, I would get to relocate to my home turf, the DC area, back to my "old stompin' ground." Another cool part of the job was that it involved a lot of fun travel around the Mid-Atlantic Region, including to Puerto Rico, which would be part of this job's territory. My excitement kept growing!

Up to this point in my life, I'm not sure there was anything I had ever wanted more. One of the main qualifications required for the position was to be an expert at speaking to large groups. I put my resume in with what I was told were hundreds of other applicants' resumes. You can imagine my utter joy and surprise when the Director that was interviewing and hiring for this position was someone familiar with my speaking ability.

Indeed, it was Bob Brinker, the Eastern Regional Training Director who had organized the event where I had stepped up to replace the missing speaker. Bob knew my skills firsthand and hired me. He would be my new boss. He said the confidence I had shown in stepping up that day had convinced him I could do the job. I went on to work for Bob until I left Pfizer, in what was, up till then, my favorite job ever.

Just Jump

Sometimes you need to just jump without thinking, like how, on my way back from the bathroom I had decided to jump on stage to speak to an auditorium full of my colleagues, or how I literally jumped into my first swim race, as you'll see up next. Stories are an ideal way to demonstrate a concept, and these ones about jumping in when you're not prepared illustrate that you won't always get the time to practice as much as you need to. Sometimes your confidence is the result of your gift, your flow, or whatever you're drawn to, like a prodigy. Other times, it simply feels like you've been struck by a lightning bolt of confidence and you just have to do it. Besides these two personal anecdotes on jumping in, this chapter is chocked full of stories of *Confidence Carriers*. Isn't it inspirational to hear tales of folks who walk in with their heads high and shoulders strong, resolute and ready, and *own it*?! Be prepared to be inspired.

Dock Dive Near Drowning

Let's take a trip back in time to my first ever swim race.

I am four years old, and it is the Labor Day Regatta Swimming Championships at Lake Barcroft. This was the place where I and many great swimmers in the Northern Virginia area learned to swim. The shore started at zero-depth and then the water got deeper—two feet, three, six, ten, and finally 20 feet deep.

I want you to visualize this calm, beautiful, pristine lake with a white sandy beach. Out in the middle of the lake are two long docks with lane ropes strung between them to form eight lanes. These were diving docks. It was about 20 feet deep out there, so the docks were quite profound. This was essentially a swimming pool in the middle of a lake, and it was about 25 yards offshore.

During the Labor Day festival, they had lots of fun events. There were penny piles where kids dug for coins in big piles of sand. Back then, they had a beauty pageant and a muscle-man contest to see who could lift the most. They also had three-legged races as well as swimming races in the offshore-dock pool.

I'm there running around with my parents and three brothers. It's mass hysteria and there are hundreds of people. I'm a tiny child watching the races in the lake. I don't know how to swim. I've never even had a swimming lesson at this point.

My brothers are off digging in sand piles as I watch the starter intently. He's got a gun and he instructs the swimmers to take their mark. The gun goes off and the swimmers jump in and start swimming. As I'm watching the flow of this, I realize that they're getting the swimmers out to the dock by ferry. There's a little rowboat with lifeguards and some big flat-bottom rowboats taking kids out for the heats.

I see kids that look about my size or a little bigger, so I line up with them at the shore, then get in the boat and ride on out there. At this point, my parents tell me that they started to freak out because they realized that I'm missing. Then they suddenly spot me in the boat getting onto the dock. I see the other kids lining up and I get in a lane. I'm thinking to myself, *Well, let's see what they're doing. They're bending over. They're curling their toes around the edge.* I hear the starter saying, "Take your mark." As I fling myself into the water, the small issue of not knowing how to swim does not enter my mind.

I had thought that maybe if a bird could fly, then I could swim—but I could not. I started to sink to the bottom of the lake, just before the lifeguard jumped in and dragged me up. I ended up being fine but not before I choked on water and scared everyone watching. They put me in the boat and brought me back to shore. For my effort, I was given a beautiful little ribbon. Over decades of competing I have won many awards including ribbons, medals, and trophies, but I never keep them. I'm a minimalist. I have, however, kept that silky, blue ribbon from my first ever swim race.

I've kept the ribbon because it reminds me of being inspired to become a swimmer. It was as if I was struck by lightning to go and enter that race. I was inspired and have not lost that passion for swimming in over 50 years. This isn't about bungee jumping, cliff diving, or doing something wild or dangerous just for the sake of it. It's about when you think you can do something and are *called* to do it—and sometimes you *do* swim instead of sink. Either way, you come out better for it.

Believe in Yourself

Whatever we want to do well in life, we feel confident towards it. It may be the first thing that comes to mind when you think about mindset. Mindset is confidence, and confidence is a mindset. It is your inner voice that matters. The famous quote that describes it best is attributed to Henry Ford: **"Whether you believe you can or you can't, you're**

right." In other words, whether you tell yourself you can do it or you can't, it's the truth. Confidence has a lot to do with your mindset and your self-talk—that ever-present voice in your head. That voice is powerful, so make sure it's supporting you and not the opposite.

Pose Confidently

As a leader or in your daily life, your posture can have a dramatic effect on your confidence. One way to describe this is "power posing." Putting your body in a straight, confident position actually changes the cortisol and testosterone levels in the brain, and these hormones play a direct role in how we feel. Think about how differently you feel about yourself if you are slumped over versus sitting, standing, or walking with your shoulders back. Try it now. In fact, a study entitled *Body Posture Affects Confidence in Your Own Thoughts* is one of many works of research to point this out. (Brinol, Petty, & Wagner, 2009; see Notes.) If you want to be more confident, start by carrying yourself with assurance.

A Tale of Two Sara(h)s

When I was the women's head swimming coach for the USC Gamecocks, I was a very passionate recruiter. In the five years that I was there, all my recruiting classes were ranked in the top 20.

We had some solid recruits coming in, and I had a special way of figuring out whether they would be a top swimmer in the NCAA. At the NCAA D1 level, and especially being in the elite Southeastern Conference (SEC), it was paramount to get recruits that could compete at the highest level. At the time, Georgia was the women's NCAA overall champion while several other programs like Tennessee, Auburn, Alabama, Kentucky, and Arkansas were all seriously competitive too.

It was possible to finish seventh in the SEC but still finish top ten or 15 in the NCAA. I knew that to compete in that conference, I had to get the best recruits. I would go after the blue-chip athletes—the highest-ranked high school swimmers who were looking at the top five Division One schools. I even got a few of those recruits away from the powerhouses.

During a visit, we would have recruits on campus for a weekend. Once we had the chance to know them a little, I would sit with them in my office at the end of their stay. I can still see my fluorescent-lit office, the chair in front of my desk for guests, and the Gamecocks posters on the wall. At that point, I would always ask them one specific question.

"I want you to imagine that you are in the final of the NCAA. You're at the NCAA championships, there are eight lanes, and you're in one of those lanes. You're up there getting ready to swim. What is going through your mind?"

Then I would be quiet and wait for their answer. You'd be amazed at the answers I got. Most of the recruits would say, "I don't know. I don't even know if I'm going to make the NCAAs. That's pretty fast. I've never swum at that level before." These are the incredible things they would say to themselves before realizing that they were talking to the woman who could give them a full scholarship—or not. But they were still truthful about what was in their mind because my question had caught them off guard.

However, one of those recruits named Sara Henninger (from Chapter 3, *Vibrant Visionary*) answered the question exceptionally well. She said, "I'm going to win. I'm going to kick butt and dominate. I'm so happy to be at NCAAs. I'm so excited, Coach! I want to get there now." This particular Sara came in as one of my first top athletes. She was out of a small program in Beavercreek, Ohio.

In her career at South Carolina, she just improved and improved and improved, and went on to be a multiple-time NCAA All-American. She performed at the level that she saw herself performing at in her mind. This is why I think that self-talk and confidence are necessary to succeed in life. In swimming, you need to be standing behind the blocks saying, "I can do this. I'm strong, I'm fit, and I'm fast."

But how did Sara get to the point where she could answer that question so enthusiastically without skipping a beat? Why was she so confident? I believe that she could see herself as the best because she had confident self-talk. Her internal voice matched what she wanted to accomplish. Does what you tell yourself correspond to who you want to be?

Confidence and mental self-talk can also come in the form of being neutral, landing anywhere between *I'm the best and I'm going to crush this,* and *I stink at this and I'm going to completely fail.* Sometimes when we're in a difficult place we cannot find the ability to tell ourselves anything encouraging. That's when neutrality steps in to save the day. You could tell yourself *I'm actually enjoying the process,* or *Gosh, the sky sure is blue,* both of which are much better options than negative self-talk. I like to refer to neutrality in this case as "thinking swimmingly." Swimmingly is a word I love not only because it incorporates swimming, but because it means smoothly, calmly, or satisfactorily. It's like a beautiful, placid lake. You're not surfing the rad waves and you're not in a dead pool of darkness. You're just in a calm place, swimmingly.

This brings me to the story of another of my Gamecock swimmers, Sarah Teske, who always had a smile on her face and was a joy to coach. Sarah was a 200 butterflier, who swam what was considered one of the most grueling and painful races in swimming. Athletes who swim the 200 fly are known to be tough, and at this big conference meet, Sarah swam her best time in this event. When she got out of the pool, she came over to me and said, "Oh my gosh! That was the best I've ever felt during a 200 fly!"

She told me how much she'd been hurting in the last 50 yards of the race. "Coach, I stayed mentally neutral and it helped me. I just couldn't say anything positive to myself. I was in so much pain, I just couldn't. So I just said to myself, *I have straight white teeth.*"

Instead of saying negative things, like how her arms and legs were hurting, or how she was fatiguing in her race, Sarah simply repeated "I have straight white teeth." That's a great use of neutrality and thinking swimmingly. Saying something neutral as part of your mental self-talk is much better than anything negative. **Confidence comes from the voice in your head, so make sure it's positive—or at least neutral.**

Prepare to Get Lucky

Bob Bowman has such rich experiences, we heard from him back in the *Passionate Persister* and *Habit Hacker* chapters. Here's another story from Bob about how preparation and confidence played into the run up to Michael Phelps' eight gold medals in Beijing. He said, "I had the advantage of knowing that this wasn't just like any week in China. This was 12 years of Michael's career leading up to it. We had worked step by step by step to get him to a point where he might have the opportunity to do this thing. And one of the things that I think made it successful is that I knew he was completely prepared. And that gave us confidence. There was not one more thing we could have done. So we just let the chips fall where they may. We can't determine how fast other people are going to swim. We can't determine how the French are going to swim their relay. We can just have him be as ready as he can be. And we were there and I told him beforehand, *You know, we hardly ever talked about winning eight, but if somebody is going to win eight, you're going to have to be 100% prepared, which you are. And you're going to have to have a little bit of luck, because winning all the relays presents a lot of variables.* We did get lucky—twice, to be honest. And after that first relay, I turned to Frank Busch and said, *Well, we used up all our luck. We're going to have to do it on our own now because that's as lucky as you can get.*"

Bob's remark about luck reminds me of a phrase whose origin is unknown yet gets straight to the point. **Luck = Preparation + Opportunity.** Its meaning is so valuable that I had it professionally painted on the Gamecock women's locker room wall. I'd say Michael Phelps did have some luck in Beijing, but that luck would not have been available to him without massive preparation.

CPR-O to Revive Your Confidence

According to Olympic Coach Greg Meehan, confidence is a skill that can be built—and I couldn't agree more. In fact, I've created my own four-step process to help do just that, *CPR-O.* Think of this acronym as giving you the tools to turn you into a confidence *pro.* CPR normally stands for cardiopulmonary resuscitation, so let's play off that to kickstart your confidence. CPR-O here means: Celebrate, Practice, Role Models, and Own It.

Celebrate Yourself and Your Confidence

The C in CPR-O reminds you to celebrate yourself *and* your confidence. When you're aiming for high goals and high achievements, you tend to set high standards, and that's normal. Let's say you're going through arduous training for something, or you're in the process of completing a big project. Maybe you're trying to start a new business or become the best person you can be. When you have high standards, it's easy to scrutinize yourself and the things you do, or didn't do. This causes perfectionism, and nobody's perfect. We beat ourselves up, "I didn't do that exactly right," or ask, "Could I have done this better?" The truth is that we could always have done something better—always.

Maybe you didn't do everything perfectly, but celebrating your small successes gives you the idea that you're succeeding. And succeeding brings on confidence.

Practice (Again)

Now we've got P for practice, although it could just as well stand for preparation. Think of practice and preparation as one—because they really are. We talked about the importance of practice in Chapter 7, the *Peak Performer*, and it's equally important for self-assurance, so get out there and practice, practice, practice! If you want to be good at something you've never done before, you have to practice it. Then once you've done it, you'll improve and gain confidence. It's as simple as that.

Role Models

R stands for role models. This is one step that is most useful when you are trying to achieve extraordinary things, like breaking the mold. Let's say that you want to make X number of dollars in a business, or you want to perform a certain way. Maybe you want to be a certain kind of person. The kind of person that can lose 20 pounds and keep it off. The kind of person that can start their own business and bring it to great heights. To achieve these things, you need to have role models to inspire you.

When it comes to breaking barriers, everyone talks about the case of Roger Bannister. Once he was the first person to break the four-minute barrier in running the mile, many more people did it the very next year. Once celebrity Olympic Champion Katie Ledecky accomplishes an incredible feat and swims the 1,500 in under 15 minutes, then more women are going to think that it's possible. Having a role model—somebody who's done it—and seeing that it's humanly possible gives you the confidence to believe that you can do it too.

In a distant way, I like to think I was a role model for the role models of Katie Ledecky. Katie and I both grew up swimming in the DC area and have both held the Potomac Valley Swimming Women's records in the 400- and 1,500-meter freestyles, only decades apart. It's amazing how the roles and models of grit and excellence are passed down through generations.

Own It

And finally, the O reminds us to own it. The phrase "owning it" is such a powerful couple of words when it comes to confidence. But what exactly does it mean? Think of it in terms of having the home team advantage. When teams play at home they have the advantage of knowing their environment, *fully*. They're comfortable with what they're doing and self-assured. *Confidence Carriers* own their worlds.

At the Women's 2021 NCAA Swimming Championships, in Greensboro, NC, there were two historic performances by the University of Virginia (UVA) and NC State University teams. They finished first and second, respectively, unprecedented for both teams. I believe this was partly because both teams felt the "home team" advantage. This event was held in a pool they had each swum in many times, and right before the NCAAs at their conference championships. I was happy for UVA to win, having grown up in Virginia and with many family and friends who are UVA alumni, but my heart was all in for my alma mater NC State and I wrote them the following letter.

Dear Wolfpack Women,

NCAAs are the most exciting time of the season, where you get to put it all on the line. Own it.

It's a privilege. Own it.

Be grateful. Own it.

You are at the top of your game. Own it.

You've trained hard, you're fierce. Own it.

This week you are in your home pool. You intimately know the water, every wall, every block, every black line and backstroke flag. Own it.

You've prepared all year and endured the challenges of Covid. You are tough. Own it.

You're as ready as you can be and that's all you need. Own it.

You are a family, with sisters to support and who support you. Own it.

You are a wolf, hungry to swim fast and devour your competition. Own it.

You are the real Wolfpack! OWN IT.   *—Kelly P*

The UVA and NC State women swimmers sure did *own it* during the NCAAs! And isn't it interesting that, if you play around with the letters that make up the word *own*, you get *won*...

And That's Just One Side of Me

Sometimes you do hit the note that wins *Britain's Got Talent (BGT)*. Susan Boyle is one of my favorite heroes for confidence. When she went out on stage for her first audition on BGT, Judge Simon Cowell asked her, "How old are you Susan?" She replied that she was 47 and did so confidently. Then Simon rolled his eyes and made a doubtful face. Susan added, "And that's just one side of me!" He continued to ask her in a doubting way, "And why hasn't it worked out for you?" "I've never been given the opportunity," she exclaimed.

Unless you've been living under a rock, then you know that Susan Boyle absolutely nailed her audition of *I Dreamed a Dream*, which the judges described as extraordinary, stunning, a gigantic wake-up call. Susan owned it out there, and the crowd gave her a standing ovation. It was Susan's confidence that spoke so loudly to me. If you ever need a boost of inspiration when you are feeling too old or like your shot hasn't come up yet, pull up Susan Boyle's original audition for BGT for a terrific role model of someone who took the leap.

Don't get me wrong. I think it's important to have a pile of preparation and past success to lean on. It's valuable to have role models. But sometimes you can just have confidence in something you've never done or done much of professionally, like Susan Boyle. You don't know why you have confidence, but you just do, and you go out there and it works. My first little swimming race at age four didn't work for me, but I know some cases that do work out. I want to put this out there: **It's possible to have confidence just because you have it, or you pretend you have it.** Next is another story that reiterates this sentiment.

Whatever You Say Lill

Olympic Champion and world record-holding swimmer Lilly King exemplifies "being confident just because she's confident." While other athletes have had her success, they don't necessarily *own it* quite like she does. Lilly is known for being the queen of confidence. In chatting with Lilly's mom Ginny King, she relayed a story of 12-year-old Lilly. "Lilly had qualified maybe sixth or seventh in an age-group final at Fishers High School in Indiana. But all day, she kept repeating, *I'm going to win, I'm going to win, I'm going to win.* And she had already dropped four seconds in the preliminary heats. We were all thinking, *Okay sure, whatever you say Lill.* I don't think any of us really believed it, not her dad nor I, not even her coach. And I'll be darned if she didn't win!" That seems to me like taking a leap of confidence.

Sometimes you go tap that person on the shoulder and you say, "Hey, I think you're cool. Let's go get a cup of coffee." It happens. You just find confidence for whatever reason and leap.

Take Your Mark, LEAD!

Lead Yourself

Sometimes you need to fake it until you make it and just take that leap. Learn on the job; confidence will come later. Practice being confident, just because you say you are confident, and try my CPR-O exercise. Self-talk is key, and stay neutral if you can't be positive. And remember… *Confidence Carriers* use and develop a strong inner voice to power a can-do mindset and make better leaders.

Lead Others

Be the voice of confidence for those you are leading. A great leader encourages and inspires, so your work team and family need to know that you believe in them, and that you have confidence in their success. In Chapter 3, *Vibrant Visionary*, I told the stories of two great leaders, Stan Tinkham and Don Easterling, who inspired me by having confidence in me.

And don't just be a voice—*act* with confidence when leading others. Almost nothing inspires followership more than a leader who believes in themselves and the cause or people they are championing.

To be a champion *Confidence Carrier:*

- ☑ Just jump
- ☑ Believe in yourself
- ☑ Pose confidently
- ☑ CPR-O to revive your confidence
- ☑ Celebrate yourself and your confidence
- ☑ Practice and prepare
- ☑ Find a role model
- ☑ Own it

9

REFLECTIVE THINKER

Reflective Thinkers make time to look back, comprehensively, on their experiences to see how they have grown and how they can improve their life and their leadership skills to move their teams forward.

"Mindfulness is a powerful tool for improving your performance in athletics and life."

—Natalie Coughlin, 12X Olympic Medalist

Playboy Model with a Cause

When you stop and take the time to think and reflect on your life and experiences, I believe it increases the chance of finding your purpose. It certainly opens your mind to the things you care most for, or a cause you're passionate about. This is how I ended up in *Playboy* magazine.

In my final semester at NC State University, I appeared as a model in *Playboy* magazine in an annual college girl pictorial named *The Girls of the ACC* (Atlantic Coast Conference). If you're not familiar with the magazine, at that time it was known as a classy nudie publication for men. It featured naked or half-naked women and was promoted as "entertainment for men." The magazine was not racy and generally viewed as mainstream, even acceptable in mixed company. At that time there was a popularized belief—certainly among most men and probably many women as well—that for someone to be selected to appear in *Playboy*, she had to be the pinnacle of feminine, sexual beauty.

Playboy came knocking twice. The first time I was approached by them I was lifeguarding at Lake Barcroft in Falls Church, Virginia. It is a lovely lake with white sandy beaches, which I described in the last chapter as the site of my near-drowning and foray into competitive swimming. As I twirled my whistle and scanned the water in typical lifeguard repose, a man approached me, saying he was from *Playboy* magazine. He told me that *Playboy* was in the DC area looking for "Playmates" and he thought I would make an ideal centerfold. Even at 16 years old, I knew what a centerfold was. **He asked me if I'd be interested in attending a *Playboy* Open House in Georgetown. I said, "Heck no! I'm 16!"** When I shared the story with my family over dinner that night, there was speculation that the guy may have been a fraud. I couldn't be certain. I never saw him again, but that encounter and follow-up discussion stuck with me.

Five years later, I was approached by representatives from *Playboy* again. This time I was sure they were frauds, but they were, in fact, the real deal. I had a part-time job during my senior year of college, working nights as a bartender at the Hilton Hotel on Hillsborough Street in

Raleigh. I was mostly a substitute at the hotel because I was also on the Wolfpack swim team, training very seriously, and attending classes, so I had little time to spare. I would pick up shifts here and there for pocket money. The tips were excellent, and I liked the bartender's uniform of a black bowtie and vest over a white shirt.

One spring evening I was serving two gentlemen seated at the bar. I was casually chatting with them, and told them I was a senior and on the swim team at NC State. Then one of them said to me, "We're from *Playboy* magazine. We've been here for two days interviewing candidates for our upcoming *Girls of the ACC* photo spread. We've interviewed 1,500 women for ten spots, and if you'll commit to being in the feature, we'll select you right now. You don't even have to try out. It's our decision. We've been watching you and we think you're just what we're looking for." "Yeah, right!" I chuckled, "*Playboy* magazine, that's a good one!" I protested, thinking back to my first encounter with the *Playboy* recruiter my family had dubbed as a fraud. My manager, who was listening in nearby but standing several feet away, called me over to him. He told me that these men *really* were from the magazine and had been holding auditions for the last couple of days at the Hilton. He said there was a line-up of women looped around the building waiting to meet with them. I had missed all the hoopla and promotion about the event because for the last week I'd been out of town participating in the NCAA Swimming Championships. After realizing my response had been a bit rude, I walked back over to them.

"So you would really put me in *Playboy* ahead of all those other women you've interviewed?" I asked. "Yes!" they answered. "And if you'll commit to us right now, we can get the paperwork going." I have to say, this was not something I had ever aspired to do, but I thought maybe it would provide a way for me to make a statement that I strongly felt needed to be made. That statement was that a woman could be an elite-level athlete and still be thought of as feminine, with sexual beauty—just what *Playboy* brokered in. Remember that this was *way* before women athletes owned their bodies confidently, openly posing nude next to a ball in an advertisement. I had spent the better part of my swimming career fighting the image of being a "jock." I'd been told I was "too pretty to be an athlete" numerous times. And this always made me furious. I had heard many women say they avoided athletics because they didn't want to be too muscular or unattractive to men. I remember one of my girlfriends telling me she didn't want to do sports because that would make her masculine.

I recall an incident that exacerbated my fury on this point, when I was selected to be part of the National Sports Festival Competition put on by the US Olympic Committee. It was like a mini-Olympics, but with American athletes only. The US was divided into North, East, South, and West for competition purposes, and I was on the South team. We got cool uniforms and swag as part of the package. The Festival was in Syracuse, NY, and they had done a nice job of setting up an "Olympic Village," housing different sports in dormitories around the Syracuse University campus, which was mostly empty for this summertime event. They had buses to take us to our designated dorms, so I got on the bus and asked the driver to take me to the dorm where the swimmers were staying. He dropped me at the bottom of a hill and pointed up to a building. I hauled my bags up and, after a rather long day of travel, I was ready to get settled into my room and prepare for the competition the next day. When I gave my name to the person checking us in at the dorm, she told me that she didn't have me on the list and that I was in the wrong place. I had been dropped off at the *synchronized* swimmers' dorm. *Grrrr!* I dragged my bags back down to the bus stop. When the same driver picked me up again, I asked him why he'd sent me there. He said, "Well, initially I thought you were too pretty to be an athlete. Then when you said you were a swimmer, I figured synchronized swimmers are the prettiest athletes so that's where I sent you. And anyway, swimmers can't have long hair like yours, can they?" Imagine! I encountered many similar instances and attitudes like this from both men and women throughout my career as an athlete. Luckily things have been slowly changing over time.

Since I was young, one of my passions has been to get more girls and women into sports because, as an athlete, I quickly became aware of the confidence, discipline, fitness, and body positivity it gave me—not to mention everything I learned from team collaboration. I wanted to share that with other girls and help them reap the benefits too.

Now back to the bar at the Hilton. *If I posed in Playboy as a D1 NCAA All-American swimmer, then this would spread my message loud and clear. You could still be an elite athlete and be feminine and sexy.* That was my reasoning.

I told the *Playboy* scouts that I needed until the next day to decide, as I wanted to talk with my family and friends before making a final decision. I also made two non-negotiable demands. 1) That if I signed on for this, they would allow me to be in my Wolfpack team swimsuit at the competition pool at NC State. I wanted it to clearly show that I was an athlete. I would not be lying in lingerie on my dorm room bed. And 2) That I would be fully covered by my swimsuit. No nudity or semi-nudity would be involved. They agreed.

I consulted with friends, my team members, and family. Almost everyone considered it a great opportunity and encouraged me to go for it, except for my Mom. "Think of your grandmother, Mamaw," she said, but her objections weren't strong enough to stop me.

Playboy kept their promise and allowed me to be photographed at the pool in my swimsuit. The photographer was David Chan, famous for having captured hundreds of Playmates since 1968, and the make-up artist was former centerfold, Victoria Cooke. I was shocked when David told me that he thought I was the first *real* athlete ever to pose for *Playboy*. We had to do the photoshoot at 2 a.m. so the pool would be completely empty. David set up loads of professional-looking camera equipment while Victoria, who was very sweet and skilled at her job, did my make-up. It was just the three of us in a cavernous university pool. Soon the flashes were going off and I was posing in different positions, all while fully wearing my Wolfpack swimsuit. The photos were all taken in and around the lane in which I had swum thousands of yards over hundreds of hours. It was definitely an athletic setting—just what I had wanted. **As the session was coming to an end, David said, "Kelly, it's a once-in-a-lifetime event to be photographed by me and *Playboy*. Would you like to do one shot topless?** Your boyfriend or future husband might appreciate it." At this point, it was 4 a.m. and I was feeling quite cozy and trusting of David and Victoria, so I dropped my top (and only my top!) for just one click of the camera. Can you guess which photo ended up in the magazine?

The attention that followed was mind-boggling. TV interviews, tours of the Atlantic states, a trip to the Playboy mansion in Chicago. I figured if I was going to promote my cause, I would work the publicity. But I drew the line when I was offered a centerfold. I knew Mamaw could handle a topless shot, but a centerfold required full nudity. It would have paid what was a large amount to me back then, and it certainly might have changed my career trajectory, but it would not have helped my cause any more than what I'd just done. I passed.

I really didn't like all the media attention and was happy it seemed to be settling down. However, a few weeks after the magazine hit the newsstands, I got a taste of just how intrusive fame can be. I was caught off guard when shopping in my local drugstore in Raleigh. As I stood there trying to decide what brand of shampoo to buy, a young man brought me a copy of the *Playboy* with my feature, which he'd just gotten off the rack, and asked me to sign it. So I did. Other guys started to realize what was going on and they wanted me to sign their magazines, too. I think there was probably a bus with a sports team or fraternity right outside the store because I must have signed 20 magazines. Those were some of the last moments of my "15 minutes of fame." I was glad to see them go.

That event at the drugstore made me realize that I'm not a fan of fame. It felt like I had no control over my life, and that my freedom was limited. It goes without saying that freedom is one of our most precious commodities, and you often hear celebrities bemoaning their lack of it. This short encounter with some of my fans was an excellent lesson—and one I did not care to repeat.

In reflecting back on this, I believe that my *why* behind posing for *Playboy* was authentic, albeit naive. I think if I had been allowed more time to think it through, I could have found better ways to get my message across. I felt rushed by the compressed timeline to decide, and **making rushed decisions is never ideal.** I also wish I would have consulted with older, wiser women, at least one who was not my Mother. On the positive side, it was a unique sampling of the world of modeling and fashion, which I learned was not for me. On the other hand, however, I found that many people started judging me negatively for what had happened. And even worse: that *Playboy* photo got the attention of a man who became obsessed with me and stalked me for more than ten years. At one point I had to get a restraining order against him after he'd delivered gifts to my doorstep every day for a month. When I followed everyone's advice and ignored him completely, he wrote me a note saying, "It's your choice: Be with me in life or in death." How scary! Talk about loss of freedom...

After casting back through this whole experience and using it as an example for us all, I believe there are three ways to reflect on situations: through your past self, your current self, and your future self. **In looking at your past self, you can ask, *Did I make the right decision at that time?*** When evaluating past behaviors, it's important not to flagellate yourself for your actions, *if* you believe that you made the best decision you could with the information and beliefs you had at that time. At that time, my flawed belief was that my appearance in *Playboy* would assist my cause.

My current self says that there were probably much better ways to have made my point. And while *Playboy* does broker in sexual, feminine beauty, at the end of the day, it is "entertainment for men" and objectifies women, which I'm totally against. If I were able to travel back in time, I would advise my 21-year-old self to find a better way to make my point and skip posing in *Playboy*. And if I wouldn't listen to myself, then I'd advise getting more than my peer groups' opinions. Nonetheless, my present-day self also feels that all my experiences, good, bad, and ugly, have brought me to where I am today, and for that I am grateful.

And while reflection has the connotation of being oriented towards the past, I feel my story illustrates the need to look forward as well.

Looking at all points in your life, past, present, and future, is definitely one way to be mindful. So if I make it to my Dad's age, 91, I think I'll look back from my rocking chair and be pleased that I posed for *Playboy*. Maybe because I'll be senile, or maybe because I'll be utterly wise. But just maybe because at the end of our lives, **research says that we usually regret more of the things we did not do than the things we did.** (Gilovich & Husted, 1994; see Notes.)

Taking the time to reflect can help suss this out, and maybe even prevent future regrets. When you're 91, what will you wish you had done?

Share with Sage Counsel

How does this apply to leading yourself and others? There are two main reasons I included that story here. First, I believe that while feeling passionate about a cause, as leaders often do, it is incredibly valuable to share your ideas with others, especially those who can offer wisdom, experience, and an alternate point of view. Secondly, I felt it was a prime example of demonstrating the actual practice and importance of self-reflection. Looking back, I'm struck by how little thought I gave to the potential repercussions of that magazine shoot, and how my circle of advisors was utterly lacking in diverse opinions.

Write Your Review

I have never deeply reflected on what my *Playboy* experience meant in my life, until now. And I certainly have never written about it. Yet what better time to review your actions than when you are in the process of writing a book? But you don't need to be writing your grand memoir to contemplate what's happened or what's happening. Just putting your words down on paper makes your thoughts more clear. That is why daily journaling can be such a valuable tool for reflection. The stories with Matt and Ray coming up are interesting examples of reflecting and acting on those reflections.

Matt and Ray: Unfinished Business-Men

After recently interviewing Matt Biondi for this book and our podcast, I learned he is a very reflective thinker. He's also an 11X Olympic medalist and a 14X world record-holder who competed in the Olympic Games in 1984, 1988, and 1992, winning eight gold, two silver, and one bronze medal. During his heyday, Matt's star power might have rivaled that of Mark Spitz or arguably Michael Phelps. Besides being a swim star, his good looks and charismatic smile drew fans galore.

Yet Biondi's earning power was squelched by amateur rules that were patently unfair, especially to swimmers, when US Olympians from other sports were allowed greater opportunities. Part of the reason Matt left the sport of swimming and went into teaching for 17 years was the lack of financial support and opportunities for pro swimmers. Now after reflecting on his life and how he can make a difference, 30 years later he's working with the International Swimmers' Alliance (ISA). Matt is banding swimmers together in order to negotiate fair pay. He wants the ISA to be a proponent of swimmers earning equitable money and having a seat at the decision-making table for professional swimming. It's never too late to look at your life and evaluate what your highs and lows have taught you.

Ray Looze's story has a similar theme. When I sat down with Ray, Head Men's and Women's Swim Coach at Indiana University and assistant coach of the 2016 Olympic team, he said he thinks many of the best coaches have unfinished business from their own careers as swimmers. Ray finished third at the Olympic trials, missing the US Team by one place. He's gone on to coach Olympic Champions Lilly King and Cody Miller, certainly filling the gap he felt in his own history. He said in thinking about his career and a dream unfulfilled, he wanted to help others reach their goals. This is a theme in reflective thinking. **How can you turn what has happened to you into something extraordinary and possibly helpful to others?** You won't know unless you reflect on your life as Matt and Ray have.

Five Steps for Thorough Reflection

Here are five steps to reflective thinking that include both actions and questions to ask yourself. You can take these steps anytime in your life when you need to pause and assess what you've been through. Taking the time to reflect can set you up for an awesome year, season, or month to come.

1–Ritualize and Savor Some Silence

The first thing to do is to set aside 30 to 60 minutes in complete, uninterrupted silence. Silence is key. Get comfortable, sit quietly, and think. Get a notepad and just write down everything that comes to mind. Next, make it a ritual. We learned in Chapter 7, the *Habit Hacker*, that a ritual is a regular activity that has special meaning and purpose. So find your favorite spot, light a candle maybe, and create a ritual for reflecting, once a day, week, month, or year—or even better, all of the above. **If making reflection too formalized is slowing down the process, try silently reflecting in a space where you would normally listen to music, an audiobook, or a podcast.** This could be during your shower, on your daily walk, or on the drive back from dropping a friend at the airport. With all the technology we have these days, sometimes *silence is (truly) golden*. Listening to and recognizing the value of your inner thoughts is really all that reflecting comes down to.

2–How do you feel?

The first question you should ask yourself in reflecting on the past year (or period you've chosen) is how did it make you feel? What emotions come up when you look back on that year? Sadness, joy, pride, exhaustion, boredom, disappointment, frustration, surprise, happiness?

3–Where have you been?

We notice that champions reflect on their track records with extensive benefit, such as death-defying swimmer Lewis Pugh who swims in Arctic waters with predators like killer whales, leopard seals, and polar bears. Then there's endurance cyclist Jeffrey Ritter, who overcame a broken neck while cycling, to come back and win a world championship on his bike, and McKenzie Coan, a Paralympic gold medalist swimmer with brittle bone disease who has broken 65 bones in her body. While we may not have such extreme experiences like these champions who stay tough, an easier way to stay strong is to remind yourself of the tough things you've done or survived in the past. **If you have gotten through something tough before, you can certainly do it again.**

As you read this you may be going through things that are worse than all the things I've described here, but know that you can survive it. What I've learned is that you've got to keep moving. You've got to take action.

When reflecting on the activities that you did each month over the past year or season, think about what obstacles you overcame and what you learned from them. Gather up all those victories and remember them next time you start to doubt yourself. See? You *are* tougher than you thought!

4–Gain Clarity

We all have tools to help us remember what we need to do in the future and what we did in the past. Go through your calendar month-by-month and write down all that you did this year.

Are there any resources that will help you remember all you've accomplished? Even the things that you didn't put in your calendar?

My husband and I were having an argument about how much I had traveled this past year. Mark told me, "Go to *Google Timeline*. Pull it up." We did, and indeed, there were quite a number of little road trips that were on my timeline that weren't even on my calendar. Some people keep a tight calendar, but I hadn't. *Google Timeline*, an app that tracks your location, is a cool way to see everywhere you've been throughout the year and a great way to trigger reflection. An app is one resource for this example, but you can think of people as resources too. Who could you talk with, as I wish I had in my *Playboy* story, that might help you get a more accurate picture?

5–Which areas can you improve in, and where does the most impact lie?

In Chapter 4, the *Discipline Developer*, we talked about the 80/20 rule, the *Pareto Principle*, which suggests that 20% of your activities should account for 80% of your results. So ask yourself what 20% of your activities could you work on that might improve 80% of your life.

These kinds of big-ticket benefits might be such things as exercise, meditation, better sleep, or less time on screens. All of them require not nearly as much time as the payoffs they produce. What could you add that would bring you big returns?

Try these five steps for thorough self-reflection. With endless opportunities for digital distraction nowadays, it's getting even harder to contemplate our lives, so be mindful of this. Make time to delve deep inside your past, your present, and future self.

Take Your Mark, LEAD!

Lead Yourself

Through reflection, we get to see how resilient we really are. We can refocus on our goals and consciously work on improving our outlook and offering more to others.

A technique we covered in Chapter 5, *Passionate Persister*, is working on *now I am*. This is also an invaluable tool for mindfulness. Verbally complete the phrase, *now I am. Now I am journaling. Now I am breathing.* This practice is a great way to increase your enjoyment of the present moment.

We can also project ourselves into the future and contemplate that. Refer to the summary checklist below to become a champion *Reflective Thinker*. And remember... *Reflective Thinkers* make time to look back, comprehensively, on their experiences to see how they have grown and how they can improve their life and their leadership skills to move their teams forward.

Lead Others

First reflect on where your team, group or organization has been, then evaluate what is happening now. Finally, contemplate where you want to be in the future. Take your group through the same steps as you went through yourself, above. Create a comfortable, nonjudgmental quiet space where you can ask yourselves the same questions. *How do we feel individually, and as a team? What have we been through, and how could we make this ride smoother in the future? Which areas could have the most positive impact on our group?* Identify the best resources to help you get an accurate picture of where you've all been and where you're all going.

Reflect on Other Leaders

At the beginning of this book, I said that leaders are readers. They're learners. To lead others, reflect on what the leaders you admire are doing. I'm inspired and learn from all the leaders I've mentioned in this book. Start devouring podcasts, audiobooks, and *TED Talks* in your area of passion and purpose. Explore shows like *Impact Theory* and *Women of Impact*. Learn from high-performance thought leaders like Tom Bilyeu, Lisa Bilyeu, Tony Robbins, Brendon Burchard, Jim Rohn, and Mel Robbins. If you investigate what some of the best minds in your field are doing, I guarantee it will make you a better, more reflective leader.

To be a champion *Reflective Thinker:*

- ☑ Share your reflections with wise counsel

- ☑ Write your review

- ☑ Ritualize and reflect in silence

- ☑ Ask yourself, *How do I feel?*

- ☑ Ask, *Where have I been, and what have I been doing?*

- ☑ Call in resources to help create accuracy

- ☑ Where can you improve to make the most impact?

10

SUCCESS CELEBRATOR

*Success Celebrators release stress and
increase motivation by imagining a well-earned reward,
remembering their strengths, and appreciating
themselves and others.*

*"Recognize there was a great effort in the process.
Then you have to celebrate that, not just the medal around
your neck at the end, but celebrate the process too."*

—David Marsh, 2016 Head US Olympic Swim Coach

Cody Fist Pumps Bronze

One of the better celebrations I've admired from a champion on the world stage was US swimmer Cody Miller in the 2016 Olympic final of the men's 100-meter breaststroke. While some athletes, especially at the Olympic level, feel disappointed if they don't bring home the gold, Cody epitomized the *Success Celebrator* persona by honoring his third place—and for all the right reasons. Cody's bronze medal effort came behind the most notable athlete in the pool, who had dominated the race by a large margin, Adam Peaty. Peaty, whose amazing world record-breaking swim had ignited the crowd, sat atop the lane rope, post-race, waving to fans. As the camera zoomed in on Peaty, you could see and hear Cody, one lane over, proclaiming his celebration with a loud "Woo, Woo!" and a few happy fist pumps. Cody was in his own world, enjoying the fact that he had just won bronze, set an American record, a personal best time, a trip to the Olympic podium, and most likely had just earned himself a place on the US 4x100 medley relay as the breaststroker—an opportunity that would yield him a gold medal of his own. There was a lot to celebrate there, but many people might have let someone else's success cloud their own accomplishments. Not Cody.

When Cody was on the *Champion's Mojo* podcast he told us, "If I've done everything I can possibly do to prepare myself for a race and I give it my best effort, then no matter what happens, I've won." Now that's something to celebrate!

Start with Gratitude

While this chapter is about celebration, it must be said that to lead yourself and others, the practice of gratitude is of paramount importance and has been proven to enhance happiness. (Emmons & McCullough, 2003; see Notes.) As a journalist, I've conducted hundreds of interviews with champions across several walks of life. There's one value that pops up the most and that's gratitude, the state of being grateful. Gratitude allows you to feel hope, grace, and dignity in almost any situation. Champions often express gratitude for the obstacles they faced and overcame, for the gifts along their path, and for reaching the pinnacle of their desires. They express how grateful they are for parents, friends, co-workers, coaches, teachers, doctors, and more. There's a fine line between gratitude and celebration. In fact, I'd say they are twin nuggets of joy, virtually interchangeable. But to celebrate you must first have gratitude for what you are about to honor. Both are dynamic ways to boost your wellbeing and performance.

Allow me to share a letter I wrote out of gratitude and celebration.

Dear Coreena,

Last week I was diagnosed with breast cancer. As you know, it was found only on ultrasound but missed on a diagnostic mammogram. Within a two-week period, I had one diagnostic mammogram and two ultrasounds done. You (and only you) found an 8mm mass, confirmed by biopsy, that turned out to be an invasive ductal carcinoma.

Your skill and thoroughness as an ultrasound technician have most likely saved my life, or minimally saved me from a much more serious cancer. The mass that you found is extremely close to my chest wall, and if this small mass had grown, it could have invaded my chest wall and lymph nodes. After an MRI with contrast, it has been determined that the mass is not yet in my chest wall. Because of you, I can have a lumpectomy, some radiation, and be cured. I hate to think of what the difference might be if I had waited six months to a year.

When you did my ultrasound I thought that you were spending "too much time." In fact, I questioned you about that, impatiently. The first ultrasound tech (who missed the mass just two weeks before) spent five to ten minutes with me. You spent 30 minutes. Your persistence and ability to ignore my badgering allowed you to find my cancer.

What makes this a more interesting story is that I came to get an ultrasound on a larger, palpable lump, which on biopsy turned out to be benign, normal breast tissue. After you did the ultrasound on that larger lump, you found the smaller, second cancerous lump—which no one or no other test had found.

Thank you from the bottom of my heart and the hearts of my friends and family for doing your job like someone's life depends on it—because it does! We are all celebrating you for what you did for me!

Gratefully, Kelly Palace

Seven Reasons to Celebrate

There are many common celebrations in life, like birthdays, holidays, and anniversaries. As a society, we're good at those. But those are not the kind of celebrations I want to focus on in this chapter. Instead, I want to discuss how celebrating your own small or large accomplishments in your everyday life and business can make you happier, and more productive.

Celebrating your successes isn't only about crossing the finish line or getting your to-do list done. It also helps you get yourself through things that you *need* to do but don't *want* to do—like things you dread. Afterward you can say, "You know what? I did that!" That stress-relieving moment of celebration allows you to reflect on your strength.

And of course, celebration means something different to everyone. It could involve throwing a party, a day-trip to your favorite park, art gallery or museum, or spending a whole weekend curled up with your favorite book. It could mean treating yourself to a small gift, or anything else that makes you happy. (I'm partial to wind chimes.) Celebrating could even be as simple as going out for a sunset walk. Whatever the word means to you, let's explore seven benefits of incorporating it into your life.

1–Cues up Your Success Reel

Celebrating gives us a visual cue for our vision board or end-game objectives. Visualize how you're going to celebrate when you accomplish your big goal.

Think of the football end-zone dance or the winning race car drivers at the Indy 500 drinking milk as it spills all over them. At the Kentucky Derby, it's the Run for the Roses when they cover the horses with roses. As a swimmer, I think of the coaches and their whole team jumping into the deep end with their clothes on when they win the conference title or the NCAAs. That's the type of celebration you can see in your mind's eye and think, "Wow, when I do all this hard stuff, I'm going to get *that*."

A celebration is the perfect thing to visualize for your end goal. But it doesn't have to be huge, like the events I just described. You can also envision celebrating completing a project, cooking a great meal for your family, or starting an exercise program.

2–Spotlights Your Strengths

Celebrating shines the spotlight on your strengths and helps you realize "the stack" of what you have accomplished. Maria and I began using the term "stack" to remember our strengths after interviewing Lewis Pugh, who used that word to describe how he builds up his confidence before a swim in dangerous Arctic waters.

I never get tired of Lewis's wisdom and inspiration, and again, I believe he's a modern-day superhero. You learned about him in Chapter 4, the *Discipline Developer*. If you'd like more on him, his autobiography *Achieving the Impossible* is a bestseller and was chosen for Oprah's Exclusive Book List.

3–Soothes Stress

Celebrating let's off steam. When we feel pressure to achieve, stress and anxiety can build up. I'll go back to the analogy of jumping in the pool at the end of a meet. The end of a four-day swim meet is stressful. You're wound up tight and you can't release because you've got to stay focused. One of my favorite concepts from the many athletes I've talked to comes from Olympic Champion Ryan Murphy, who says that he doesn't let himself get too high or too low during meets. Staying on an even keel is important, and sometimes, doing so can build up stress. You can't cry, and you can't scream, "Wow, I just did that!"

It relieves stress when, at the *end* of the meet, you jump into the pool with your clothes on and finally shout, "We did it!"

Or you could celebrate in some way that physically relieves your stress, by going to the spa, for example. Tell yourself, "Hey, if I do six weeks of this new training program, then I'm going to treat myself to a massage."

Taking time that is not task- or goal-directed gives us the opportunity to release stress in a way that is beneficial to future goals.

4–Maximizes Motivation

Celebrating inspires and maximizes motivation, and gives us something to look forward to.

The Cheerleader with Alzheimer's

My amazing, devoted, beautiful Mother spent more hours than I can count watching me at swim practices and meets. Attending my swim meets was one of her favorite things. She rarely missed any of them from when I started at age six through to my college career. As we both aged, she would sometimes comment that she wished she could see me swim as an adult Masters swimmer. She was so proud of my accomplishments. Because we lived many miles apart she only saw me swim one Masters meet, when she was 87. That meet was held in February 2017, and she passed away in April of the next year.

The conditions that allowed her to finally see me swim again came about because I often visited my parents for weeks at a time so I could help take care of my Mom, who had been recently diagnosed with Alzheimer's. She wasn't in need of full-time care yet, but was forgetful and would sometimes leave a pot burning on the stove or forget to eat. She also had forgotten how to run the dishwasher, washer, dryer, coffee maker, and microwave, so my Dad was doing everything around the house and needed help.

Being in the Richmond, Virginia area allowed me to swim with some of my favorite Masters swimming friends and Coach Mark Kutz, who coaches with NOVA of Virginia Aquatics. Going to the pool was a huge pressure release from helping my parents and the sadness of watching my Mother deteriorate. The longer I stayed with my parents and trained with my fast friends (like Val Van Horn Pate and Chris Stevenson) and Coach Mark, the faster I got in the pool.

On the calendar several weeks out was an early February Masters meet, the VMST David Gregg III Memorial, hosted locally by NOVA. I thought it was a great opportunity for my Mom to come and see me swim. She was becoming sad from Alzheimer's, unlike her usual self. I think she sometimes realized that she was losing her mind and would cry a lot. Coming to watch me swim would be something fun for her and something we could both celebrate together.

In my usual manner of approaching a swim meet, I set some goals. At this particular meet, knowing that my Mom would be watching, I set

my goals a little loftier than usual in order to get her excited and engaged. I shared with her that I was going to try to break the national
record in the 1,000-yard freestyle.

Setting a US Masters national record is not an easy feat and I had
done it only twice before in multiple decades. While I have won many
Masters national titles, setting a national record is extremely elite.
The 1,000-yard freestyle record for my age-group, 55-59, was held
by the legendary Laura Val in a time of 11:20.53. The fastest I had
swum in the year prior was 11:31.19. I would have to drop almost 11
seconds, or 1 second per 100 to break the record. This was a challenge
for sure.

Coach Mark put me through some rough sets over the next several weeks to help me get fit enough to hit my goal of swimming under
11:20. Certainly being physically fit was important, but I also spent a lot
of time envisioning the celebration I would have with my Mom, Coach
Mark, and my teammates, if and when I did set the record. Thinking
of celebrating that record and the joy it would bring my Mom helped
motivate me.

The morning of the meet finally arrived. I had not told Coach Mark
that I was bringing my Mom to watch me, so when I burst through the
double doors of NOVA carrying a big plastic chair with Mom in tow
behind me, Mark said, "What are you doing? Are you trying to ruin your
taper carrying that thing?" I had grabbed the chair off my parent's patio
for my Mom to sit in because I knew she would be uncomfortable on
the bleachers. I set her right at the end of my lane opposite the starting
end of the pool, several feet back from the edge, but so she could still
see me clearly.

Finally, the starter said, "Take your mark," and I was on my way.
As most proficient distance swimmers do, I found my pace early and
was swimming 34 seconds for each 50, just like clockwork. This pace
was right on the edge of my threshold of being very painful, and at about
the 800-yard mark of the race I started to really hurt.

Let me paint the scene of this super low-key Masters meet. It was
very quiet on the pool deck with a sparse number of swimmers choosing
to hang around during the distance events. I didn't know if I was on pace

to set the record or not. When I glanced left and right as I swam, the pool deck looked deserted. That was until the last 100 yards, when I looked up and saw 20 or so young swimmers lining the long side of the pool all with their arms in the air, bouncing and yelling. Now I could hear and feel the roar of the 20 little swimmers cheering. I even spotted my Mom standing there cheering for me.

Coach Mark pulled a huge leadership move and saw the need to get all the volunteer swimmers that were timing behind the blocks to come and cheer me on in the last 100. He knew I was close to breaking the record, and if I had stayed on the pace I was holding, I would've missed it. I had swum all the 50-yard splits at 34 plus seconds each, but when I saw those swimmers cheering for me and envisioned celebrating with my Mom, Coach, and friends, my last two 50 splits were a 33 and a 31. I broke the national record by just 0.68 seconds.

I climbed out of the pool and fist-bumped with Coach Mark and teammates Val and Chris—I didn't want to give them wet hugs. Then I headed toward my Mom, whose smiling face glowed with joy and pride. She didn't mind a wet hug and we held each other tightly. I thanked her for being there and cheering for me. I intuitively knew that was the last time my Mom would ever see me swim. But for that moment, we celebrated.

5–Reinforces that You Rock

It's one thing to set a national record when you know what the record is. You go for it, achieve it, and use celebration for motivation. But it can also be helpful to realize obscure, or little-known reasons to motivate yourself and then celebrate. Sometimes when we are head-down, working hard on a project—which is often *just* the time when we need to stop and celebrate—it's valuable to ask, *Where am I in the grander landscape of what I'm doing?* Usually if you are diligent and keep showing up, you're going to find that yes, you do have something to celebrate.

This happened with our podcast. We recently published our 100th episode of *Champion's Mojo,* which was obviously something to celebrate. And we'd used a little-known statistic to motivate us.

Podcasting is hard work and the glamour can wear off quickly. In fact, according to Podnews.net, Todd Cochrane from *Blubrry* says that 75% of the podcasts on *Apple* are no longer in production, a phenomenon known as "podfade." (Cridland, 2018; see Notes.) Statistics show that the majority of podcasts fade out after their ninth episode. Since we first started *Champion's Mojo,* Katie and Brant Parsons have been our producer and audio engineer, respectively. We love them and they've done so much for us since episode one. We were aware of the podfade phenomenon and wanted to avoid it, so we celebrated our first ten episodes, and every ten thereafter, by giving them a Starbucks gift card to say thank you for their work. Completing ten, then 20, 30 episodes were small victories for us all. We knew that we weren't in an elite class of podcasters yet, but it was still something to celebrate and it kept our team motivated. **Aspiring to be the number one in your field is admirable, but sometimes it is important to see where you are in the grand scheme of things. And suddenly you may realize, you rock!**

Celebratory gifts and rewards don't have to be huge to inspire the motivation to go forward. Even small celebrations remind you of why you're pursuing the goal in the first place and keep you focused on your purpose and vision.

Preventable Pain

There's a community that celebrates me and they sometimes praise me, "Kelly, you rock!" This is because I helped bring awareness to a horrific condition that many suffer from, without knowing the cause. It's called Topical Steroid Withdrawal Syndrome, or TSWS, and before I could make any difference, I first had to endure TSWS myself. It was beyond dreadful.

It's hard to believe that following your doctor's orders could lead to years of such preventable misery! During my withdrawal from topical steroids, my skin turned bright red and I couldn't sleep. My body lost its ability to regulate its temperature, making me feel cold even in the heat. My skin atrophied and I got several infections. The burning and itching were unbearable, a symptom often described by sufferers as a soul-sucking itch. My skin oozed, dried, cracked, peeled, repeating this cycle over and over and over again. As TSWS flares and subsides, this nightmarish cycle can last for months up to years. Mine lasted on and off for seven years. To make it through, I lived for the good times and endured the bad times using the tools in the *Passionate Persister* chapter.

I turned to multiple dermatologists for help, who all diagnosed my condition as incurable and wanted to prescribe more steroids 'for relief.' Yet one pioneering dermatologist, Dr. Marvin Rapaport, was different. He guided me through recovery, telling me never to use topical steroids again. Dr. Rapaport says that most kids outgrow eczema, that most adult eczema can be controlled with lifestyle changes, and that perpetual, "incurable" eczema is often caused by overuse of topical steroids.

Right when I started this arduous journey, I decided I wanted to raise awareness and help others. If I had this unknown condition, who else might have it too? When I shared my story online in 2009, there was no information on TSWS out there. Then in 2012, Dr. Rapaport and I co-founded a non-profit charity called ITSAN, the International Topical Steroid Awareness Network. I did the administrative part of the process and Dr. Rapaport was the medical expert. The first few years I must have answered hundreds of emails to support caregivers and sufferers.

What has transpired since creating ITSAN almost a decade ago is nothing short of a miracle. Beyond my own journey from steroid dependence to recovery, **I discovered that *thousands of people all over the world, from infants to the elderly,* are suffering from TSWS.**

Through data from prevalence studies, it is estimated that there are 3.8 million TSWS sufferers in the US alone, and ITSAN has had people from over 50 countries join the site's online support and resources groups. (Hanifin & Reed, 2007; see Notes.) They find solutions and share success stories, which really makes my heart sing. One woman, Rochelle Richter, wrote that she "didn't want to live anymore because of the pain." Then she discovered ITSAN's resources and has since managed to heal herself 100%. Rochelle now serves on the charity's board, and there are hundreds of success stories like hers. Now that's worth celebrating!

As a champion for this cause, I'd like to share a message about the dangers of topical steroids. (Please forgive this shameless plug!) For more information on avoiding Topical Steroid Withdrawal Syndrome, visit ITSAN.org.

6–Points out the Positives

Going through TSWS could have been the lowest point in my life, and for a while I thought it was. But now I believe, from a leadership perspective, that it has been the highest point in my life, so far. And celebrating highlights these positives. We are too often drawn to the negative side of things, viewing the glass as half-empty. The news we consume is generally negative; even our self-talk can get us down. **Taking the time to celebrate gives us evidence of excellence and of the many good things going on in the world.**

7–Accents Appreciation

Celebrating shows appreciation and acceptance. When you've got a huge goal, think about who is going to be at that victory celebration with you. Who's going to walk next to you across that stage? If you're winning an Academy Award or crossing the finish line of your first marathon, who will you be thanking in person, or by email? Who's there doing a *happy dance* with you? As a leader, when you recognize others, you show your appreciation and get people motivated for the next project.

You just heard the story of my journey through topical steroid withdrawal and creating a charity to help sufferers. The timing of an achievement by ITSAN, as I write this (March 2021), could not have been more perfect for the theme of this chapter. It's big news!

That news, delivered to me by the current ITSAN President Kathy Tullos, is that the most prominent and impactful organization that can amplify ITSAN's message and mission, the National Eczema Association (NEA), has finally fully embraced us. They published an announcement on their website recognizing TSWS as a legitimate condition, along with several in-depth interviews with members of the ITSAN community. They now have a TSW information page on their website and are actually partnering with us in our efforts. This is unprecedented, and mind-blowing!

Kathy also passed along this message to me when she found out I was mentioning ITSAN in a leadership book. She wrote, "Kelly, you have such a beautiful legacy of strong female leadership following in your footsteps on the trail you blazed. You trained up leaders who trained up leaders. You broke ground and laid the foundation your successors could build upon. I think in addition to your being the co-founder and first president of ITSAN, your raising up leaders to continue on and execute your vision is a major accomplishment." So now is the perfect time to celebrate ITSAN's three presidents who came after me: Joey VanDyke, Kelly Barta and Kathy Tullos. All of these strong women are passionate, caring, determined, and patient, just to name a few of the qualities that make them ideal leaders for this cause.

When we first launched ITSAN ten years ago, the NEA called us "internet quacks," barred us from their conventions, and had my husband and I kicked out of one of their meetings in Los Angeles. I thought it might be a cold day in hell before they partnered with us. But it looks like the perseverance of the presidents mentioned above and the many, many volunteers over the last decade has finally paid off! Time for me to send out some appreciative, celebratory emails. It's *happy dance* time!

Besides the friendship that has now been built with the NEA, I'm also celebrating finishing this book. And I want to celebrate you for wanting to learn to lead like a champion. As a reward, I've written a bonus chapter called *Championing Women Leaders*.

Take Your Mark, LEAD!

Lead Yourself

Celebration requires discipline; it doesn't happen on its own. Make a plan to celebrate your small and large achievements so you can tap into all the benefits of celebration. And remember... *Success Celebrators* release stress and increase motivation by imagining a well-earned reward, remembering their strengths, and appreciating themselves and others.

Lead Others

As a leader, it is tremendously important to celebrate those you are leading. Plan an annual party or awards ceremony to recognize high performances. You would be amazed at the motivation this can give people. Obviously, this is what award banquets are for and their value is well-known. Great leaders celebrate individual and team successes.

You'll notice I closed out this chapter with my story about TSWS and ITSAN. It's one of the best illustrations of leading others and celebrations that I could write.

I hope all this will inspire you to use all the contents of this book to be a champion leader. It started off as a painful story, but in the end I championed a cause, eagerly led, made targets, vibrantly shared a vision, developed discipline, passionately persisted, used habit hacks, performed at my peak, carried myself with confidence, reflected on suffering, and celebrated the success of creating something valuable along with healing myself and others. I believe this is the greatest leadership story of my life—so far. What leadership story will you write for yourself? Now go out and live that success story! Remember to be grateful first, then celebrate.

Being a champion *Success Celebrator:*

- ☑ Cues up your success reel

- ☑ Spotlights your strengths

- ☑ Soothes stress

- ☑ Maximizes motivation

- ☑ Reinforces that you rock

- ☑ Points out the positives

- ☑ Accents appreciation

Bonus

CHAMPIONING WOMEN LEADERS

Championing women leaders is important because in doing so, everyone wins.

"Each time a woman stands up for herself, without knowing it possibly, without claiming it, she stands up for all women."

—Maya Angelou, Poet Laureate

Glass Ceilings *from* Women

The day I accepted the Head Women's Swim Coach position at the University of South Carolina in August 1990, I had no idea I was breaking a glass ceiling, of sorts. With that position I would become the first ever woman Head Swim Coach in the competitive Southeastern Swimming Conference (SEC), with such powerhouse swim schools as Georgia, Florida, Auburn, and Tennessee. It was possible to finish 7th or 8th at the SEC Championship meet and still be among the top ten or 15 schools in the country at NCAAs. I should have known that breaking this glass ceiling wouldn't be easy, but I never would have expected that my first major roadblock would come from a large group of young women.

The first day I was to meet my new team, the Gamecock women swimmers, my Associate Athletic Director, Sterling Brown, had gathered all the athletes on the pool deck bleachers to introduce me. He said, "Here's your new coach, Kelly Parker. She was an NCAA D1 All-American swimmer, has a Master's degree, five years of experience as an assistant coach at a top 20 program, and was the most qualified person for the job. She really outshined all the other candidates," he continued. He even said the words, "We did not hire her because she's a woman, we hired her because of her resume and her experience."

So my new team was sitting on the bleachers, staring at me, most of them with their arms crossed. Their body language and facial expressions were highly negative. I was wondering, *What's going on here?* Finally, before I could open my mouth, one of the team leaders, Anne Marie Wozniak, spoke up and said, "We don't want to swim for a woman."

I said, "Okay Anne Marie, thank you for your honesty. But let me ask you, what profession do you plan to go into when you graduate from here? How about you Isabel? And you Beth? Michelle?" Their answers came back: doctor, lawyer, teacher, and so on. Then I asked them all, "Do you expect your clients not to come to you because you're a woman?" I think in *that* moment, they all got it a bit and that opened the door, just a crack, for them to give me a chance.

I went on to have good relationships with the women on that team and coach successfully at USC for the next five years, earning the following honors: 24 NCAA All-Americans, three NCAA Top-25 Team finishes, 12 of 19 school records broken, ten Olympic trial qualifiers, US National Coaches List, and the number one academic team GPA in the nation with six student-athletes earning NCAA Academic All-American. The year that I left coaching for a family crisis, our incoming recruiting class was ranked as one of the best in the nation.

No Such Thing

An awkward part of being a woman coach or athlete at the University of South Carolina was their mascot, the gamecock, a fighting rooster. You can't get much more inherently male than that. Even putting the word "Lady" before Gamecock did not make being a "Lady Gamecock" any better—it was even more confusing. Historically, the NCAA and college athletics in general were for men only, and a mascot like the gamecock reflects that. Another school I worked at was the University of Arkansas, whose mascot is the razorback, most often called "The Hogs" by teams and fans. Maybe this wasn't the best mascot for female athletes either?

But less than ideal mascots aside, women moving into the NCAA was a game changer. Did you know that, initially, women's collegiate athletics weren't part of the NCAA? Women used to compete at the college level in the Association for Intercollegiate Athletics for Women (AIAW), which was disbanded in 1983. With the introduction of Title IX in 1972, women were slowly given the opportunities to participate in sports. Many people, including myself, feel this was key in creating more women leaders—though there are still not nearly enough.

Where are the Women Leaders?

When I sat down to write this chapter, I wanted to address my own thoughts and experiences on why, in the arenas I have walked and currently walk, there are so few women leaders. As I approach 40 years of experience as a woman leader, I felt my own ideas and observations might be valuable. Added to that, I've done some research, pulled some stats on women leaders, and consulted with experts who study this subject. For the most part, I want this chapter to do what the title says, and that is give anyone reading it, of either gender, some tools to champion more women into leadership positions. So let's begin with some good news.

Strides are being made with the newly launched International Swimming League (ISL), which broke barriers in 2019 by hiring two of the only women general managers in all professional sports, Tina Andrew of the New York Breakers and Kaitlin Sandeno of the DC Trident. This also makes me celebrate Teri McKeever, Head Women's swim coach at University of California at Berkeley, who became the first ever female US Olympic Swim Team Head Coach, earning this honor at the 2012 Olympics.

But women are still tremendously underrepresented in the C-Suites. According to *Fortune* magazine, "The number of women running America's largest corporations has hit a new high: 37 of the companies on the 2020 *Fortune* 500 are led by female CEOs. The *Fortune* 500, which ranks America's largest companies, has long been seen as a microcosm of US business at large. For that reason, the number of female chief executives on the list is a closely watched statistic among those who track gender diversity in boardrooms and C-suites across the country." (Hinchliffe, 2020; see Notes.)

That's only 7% of *Fortune* 500 companies that are headed up by women. In my area of expertise, NCAA D1 women's swimming, women are doing a little better than the C-Suite of corporations, but only percentage-wise. Currently only 16% of 193 D1 swim teams have women coaches *coaching women*. The number is much lower for women coaching men swimmers. And note when I say "only percentage-wise" are women swim coaches currently doing better than *Fortune* 500 companies—at least the *Fortune* list grew from 6% women CEOs last year to 7% this year.

In looking deeper into the swim coaching realm, the percentage has decreased since the 1990s. At the time of writing this book, there are only three women swim coaches of women's teams in top 20 programs. In 1995, there were six women coaches in the top 20. (Hart, 2019; see Notes.)

Making of a Leader

Elizabeth Beisel is a leader, a 3X Olympic swimmer, Olympic Team Captain, silver medalist, and author of the book *Silver Lining,* released in February of 2020. She is also a multiple NCAA Champion for the University of Florida. Now retired from swimming, she is a sports commentator and has appeared on CBS's *Survivor* television show. I interviewed her on *Champion's Mojo*, and I am thrilled to share one of her stories.

One of the greatest obstacles that Elizabeth has faced was feeling like she didn't fit in. "I made my first national team when I was 13 years old. It's no one's fault, but I was an eighth grader in middle school, so how was I supposed to relate to people who are in their twenties? And how could they relate to me? I remember absolutely hating my first few years on the national team. I felt like I didn't belong."

"Wow, I'm 13 and I'm at the World Championships. That's amazing! But I don't have friends. I don't feel like I fit in. I was so confused. So that was the moment I said to myself, *If I'm ever in a position to be an older swimmer, a veteran and a leader, I'm going to make sure that every single person feels included.* That time in my career really had an impact on me."

"Then [veteran and Olympic Champion] Natalie Coughlin, who was on my first ever national team, came and sat down with me for 45 minutes and she made me feel included. I remember thinking that was the move of a leader. *One day I'm going to be like Natalie,* I told myself. She really left a mark on me in the best way possible."

The experience helped shape Elizabeth into a leader. She stuck to her word and went on to be an Olympic Team Captain who is known for being an inclusive, caring leader. She says, **"That was the moment where this leader concept really solidified for me."**

Ten Concepts for Change

While I believe more diversity in all leadership positions is needed, this chapter is focused on women, with the exception of this first concept on bias. The list below contains some of my own unique ideas and some that have been curated from thought leaders on this subject. I hope they will inspire you.

1–Check your (Un)Conscious Bias

The story about the Gamecock women's team illustrates gender bias—my first point on ways we can champion women leaders. Get rid of gender bias. Unconscious gender bias is defined as unintentional and automatic mental associations based on gender, stemming from traditions, norms, values, culture and/or experience. Automatic associations feed into decision-making, enabling a quick assessment of an individual according to gender and gender stereotypes. We can do better than that!

Of course bias is not limited to gender. I've learned that the more we can embrace diversity, the better. It still blows my mind that the US has never had a woman President. Black men are even more rare than women when it comes to executive positions in *Fortune* 500 companies. (Brooks, 2019; see Notes.) However, there are four Black male leaders in my life who have had a great positive impact on my success. They are Harold White, an Associate Athletic Director at the University of South Carolina, Steve Smith, the HR Director for Pfizer who facilitated my hiring, Everett Cunningham, my first trainer in Pfizer, and the hero leader from my 9/11 story in Chapter 1, a veritable *Eager Leader*, Everton Cranston. Each one of these leaders were exemplary. And with all the superb leaders I've had in my life, the absolute finest was my first district manager in Pfizer, Basil Klosteridis. Basil did not look like your typical leader. According to researcher Nancy Blaker, her findings suggest that tall individuals have an advantage over short ones in terms of leadership. (Blaker, 2013; see Notes.) I'm not sure how tall Basil is, but I stand at 5'7" and his height is less than mine. He's a man of small physical stature but of confident bearing and enormous positive presence. Basil was a giant in leading our team to many awards, and was truly the greatest leader I have yet to work for. My point is that if I had been turned off to these amazing humans' uniquenesses and seen only that they were not typical, I would have missed out on more than I can imagine. Women in leadership roles are currently not typical, but don't allow that to become a bias—or you could seriously miss out.

2–Start Young Girls in Sports

Elizabeth's Beisel's story is an excellent illustration of a woman leader developing through sports and being inspired by a role model. Getting young girls to participate in sports, and keeping them there, is grassroots for developing future women leaders. Sports are a natural and fun way to develop confidence, teamwork, and leadership skills. A survey of executive women found that 80% played sports growing up, and 69% said sports helped them develop leadership skills that contributed to their professional success. These stats appear in *From Locker Room to the Boardroom: A Survey on Sports in the Lives of Women Business Executives*, published by MassMutual Financial. (See Notes.)

Courtney Shealy Hart is one of only a few women currently coaching *men* at the D1 level. She is truly a pioneer and making history in this role. She is also an Olympic Champion swimmer and former pro volleyball player. Courtney gives credit for her strong leadership skills from her foundation in athletics. "I am a product of a lifetime of competitive athletics," she says, "and I can honestly and truly say that athletics changed my life. They gave me purpose and the skills of work ethic, teamwork, discipline, and leadership, which I have now translated into a career that I love."

3–Spotlight Women Leaders

Women need to see other women in leadership roles. They need to talk and hear about them *being women* and how they deal with women's differences. It's frustrating when I hear a woman say, "I don't want to be thought of as a woman president/coach/CEO"—you fill in the blank.

A Slap in the Face

As you know by now, I was a top sales producer at Pfizer pharmaceuticals. A reward for winning sales reps was to get reserved seating up front at big company meetings. The front row seats were a prime position because after anyone from the leadership team spoke, they came off the stage and greeted the audience. It was an ideal way for ambitious, competitive salespeople to get their faces known by upper management. At one particularly large meeting, the main speaker was our President of the Pharmaceuticals Group, Karen L. Katen. At the time Karen was the only woman out of the several executive branches of Pfizer. I was thrilled at the rare opportunity to see her speak and meet a woman who had made her way to the very top of a *Fortune 100* company. I couldn't be more impressed—she was our President! Her popularity was apparent and there were several people, men and women, wanting to meet her as she came off the stage. I was third in line and as I was standing there, I thought of what I might say. *Perfect,* I decided. *I'll tell her how inspired I am to see a woman in her position!* This was how I genuinely felt.

My turn arrived and I stepped up to shake her hand, saying, "Hi Karen, it's a pleasure to meet you. I'm Kelly Parker. I have to tell you how inspirational it is to see a woman president!" I don't think I would have felt any worse if she had physically slapped me across the face, because the way she responded to me was a proverbial slap. "I don't want to be thought of as a woman president, just a president," she loudly told me, with a scowl. The people waiting closely in line behind me certainly heard the commotion and I was shocked and embarrassed. Tears filled my eyes as I backed away, silently.

Dr. Kellie McElhaney, the Founder and Executive Director of the Center for Equity, Gender and Leadership (EGAL), Haas School of Business at the University of California, Berkeley, says that, **"By denying that we are women leaders we are making women unseen. It's flawed thinking."**

We need women to get away from this attitude of not wanting to be called a woman coach or a woman president. Until women have 50% of leadership positions or more, we need to address our different needs and recognize women in these roles as role models. Everyone needs role models and if we aren't allowed to say "woman leader" then we deny that capacity.

4–Broach the Subject of Support

If women leaders are going to succeed, they need to have a supportive partner. When women are headed into a demanding leadership role, they need to openly share their concerns with their partner and pre-plan so that both people in the relationship can successfully sustain a career along with their relationship. In her book, *Lean In: Women, Work, and the Will to Lead*, Facebook CEO Sheryl Sandberg says that having a supportive partner is key in climbing the leadership ladder.

5–See Kids as Not Just a Woman's Issue

In her book, *Work PAUSE Thrive: How to Pause For Parenthood Without Killing Your Career*, entrepreneur and journalist Lisen Stromberg surveyed 1,500 college-educated women with children. Of these women, 72% had paused their careers, with the vast majority stepping out of the workforce after having children because they didn't have the maternity leave they needed. According to Forbes.com, over the past few decades, the US female labor participation rate has stagnated to the point that we've fallen far behind other industrialized nations. As of 2016, the US ranks 20th in the top 22 OECD economies. According to a report from S&P Global, if women entered and stayed in the American workforce at the same pace as Norway, for example, we would add $1.6 trillion to the US economy. (Kerpen, 2019; see Notes.)

Today's workplaces are witnessing collaboration across genders and generations—and between employees and employers—in order to create solutions that work for everyone. When companies begin to provide more and better childcare and we can all agree that caring for children is a job to be shared equally, **and not just for mothers, women will be afforded more time and more opportunities for leadership.**

6–Find a Champion of Either Gender

For this section, you can use the words champion and mentor interchangeably. A mentor will champion you. One thing I've learned is that a good mentor can be hard to come by. The field can be limited based on many factors, but if you are only looking for a woman leader to be your mentor, then I think you could be selling yourself short. There is already such a small number of women leaders that finding one to mentor you makes for a very short list.

Every one of my mentors has been a man, because that is who was available to me. You can learn leadership skills from a solid leader regardless of whether they are like you. A great example of this, close to home in the swimming community, is Head Swim Coach Jack Bauerle from the University of Georgia. Jack has mentored two of the only head women's swimming coaches (at top 25 programs) in the nation. They are Carol Capitani at the University of Texas, who was one of Jack's assistant coaches, and Courtney Shealy Hart, who swam for Jack at the University of Georgia. It just takes someone who is willing to take the role of mentor.

Other leaders from the sport of swimming are working with young women as mentors, including three Olympians: Kara Lynn Joyce of Lead Sports Co. (leadsportsco.com), and Rebecca Soni and Caroline Burkle with RISE (rise-athletes.com). Programs like these based on leadership and mentoring are needed in all sports and industries to increase the number of women leaders.

7–Stop the Mean Girls

If you witness girls not supporting one another, firsthand or otherwise, then step in, offer support, and education. Former US Secretary of State Madeleine Albright, who participated in sports as a child, said, **"There is a special place in hell for women who don't support other women."**

They're Called Pigtails for a Reason

In Chapter 3, *Vibrant Visionary*, I wrote about my trip to the Olympic Training Center for an elite distance camp. As I mentioned, I had an excellent performance at that camp and beat some people that didn't like to be beaten, including a group of three girls that I would call a clique. These girls were openly bullying me. They "accidently" knocked over my drink at the training table and openly made fun of my hairstyle. "Kelly, don't you know that braids went out of fashion about ten years ago? And they're called 'pigtails' for a reason." In short, they tried everything to make my camp an unpleasant experience.

Fortunately, there were strong leaders that witnessed this and stepped in to help. Jim and Bev Montrella were two of the coaches on staff and they called a meeting with the three bullies and me. Jim asked them, "What's going on here? I see the way you're treating Kelly. Has she done something to deserve this?" "No," replied one of the girls, "we just think she gets all the attention, and it's not fair." I remember Jim saying, "Well, Kelly works very hard in practice. Maybe you should emulate her." Of course that didn't sit well with the mean girls. At the next camp meeting, where there were about 30 girls and boys, the three bullies walked into the meeting all wearing their hair braided in pigtails like mine. All the swimmers in the room laughed, which I felt was directed at me. But what does a 15-year-old girl know? I do know my face turned bright red and I wished I hadn't been wearing pigtails right then.

Jim and Bev did not like their response to the recommendation for them to emulate me. They met with the clique after the meeting, and I was informed that the mean girls had been put on "probation." They did not bother me for the rest of the camp.

Maybe you are asking yourself, *How is a story about mean teenage girls pertinent to women in leadership?* If we are going to start girls in sports at a young age so that they can develop a good self-image, positive body-image, teamwork skills, and the many other benefits of sports, then we need to have a conversation about competitiveness. In my experience, sports help develop the trait of competitiveness, though sometimes to an extreme. And in sports as in life, women often see each other as enemies because they are vying for the same trophy or job promotion. But if we can convey to young women that there are greater benefits in supporting one another than not, we can help create an environment where women collaborate and empower one another. Some of the toughest athletes that battle it out in competition are close friends outside of sports. They share ideas for training and reaching new heights. It adds a strong mental health advantage that is so important for women as they strive to make a mark for themselves.

Two of the US's top individual medley swimmers, Ella Eastin and Madisyn Cox, are direct competitors for making our Olympic team. Yes, when they are swimming they are fighting to see who will get to the wall first. I learned during interviews with each of them that out of the pool, however, they are close friends. They told me their friendship makes them better people as well as better athletes. So next time a woman beats you at something, whether that's a race or a promotion, try befriending her instead of seeing her as an adversary. I guarantee that if you've been in a contest with her, you already have something in common. And as they say, it might be the beginning of a beautiful friendship. As more and more women take the reins of leadership, it will benefit us all if we have this mindset.

From Frenemies to Friends

There's a unique paradigm propagated by Shalane Flanagan that would benefit all women—if only they embraced it. It's so groundbreaking that it's been called the *Shalane Flanagan Effect*. (Crouse, 2017; see Notes.) Instead of acting like a frenemy towards other women, you genuinely see them as friends and support their careers, pushing and pulling them alongside you to the top. You serve as a hand up for the careers of other women with whom you work, while moving yourself forward too. Shalane believes that raising other women up is rewarding and can actually be an act of self-interest. "It's not so lonely at the top if you bring others along," she says.

Shalane Flanagan made the US 2016 Olympic team and won the New York City Marathon in 2017, becoming the first American woman to win in 40 years, in an astonishing time of 2 hours 26 minutes. But to accomplish these feats, Shalane didn't train by herself, like most distance runners do. She invited, nurtured, and befriended almost a dozen of the best women runners from around the world, who came to train with her. This was unprecedented in the world of professional distance running. But it paid off for Flanagan and all the women in her group. All eleven of her training partners made it to the Olympics along with her.

Flanagan does not just talk about supporting other women; she supports them. And they all win.

8–Champion All Roles Women Choose

Whether a woman chooses to be a stay-at-home Mom or a child-free corporate ladder climber—or both, maybe just at different times in her life—we must accept all of these roles as okay. For decades, Maria was a stay-at-home Mom. Then when her kids left the house, she embraced her business side and is now the CEO of a successful bike company.

"You can have it all. You just can't have it all at the same time," she says. "Give yourself a break. There are seasons in our lives for all things. There can be a season to be a Mom and a season when that need will be filled and you can do something else, if you choose."

Sometimes it seems that women are our worst enemies, like my own initial team at the University of South Carolina, who didn't want to swim for a woman. I've heard some women who have chosen to focus on their career say about women who stay at home, "Oh, she's just a Mom," or "She's just a housewife." And in the same vein, I've heard women be called the derogatory acronym, COB (career-oriented b*tch) by women who stay at home with kids. The point is that no role is more valuable or better than the other. Women need the right to choose and not feel persecuted or judged for their choice—especially not by other women.

9–Have a Parachute

Some people might think leading is as scary as skydiving. And if you do, would you ever go skydiving without a parachute? Of course not. So if you are absolutely terrified of leading, then have a proverbial parachute, or a back-up plan, in case something goes wrong.

For the last year I've led a weekly women's group via Zoom. I'm still in the group, but have stepped down as the leader. In order to fill that gap, we decided to rotate the leader position each week. One woman consistently did not want to perform in this leadership position. There was no pressure on her, nor did any of us mind each week when it was her turn and she declined. Finally, she opened up one day—after several months!—and told us that she was terrified of talking to groups, even our smallish online group, and that she would physically start to shake. We all encouraged her by saying, "If you start to guide us and it's too much for you, then one of us will help out." She seemed very relieved at this. One of us stepping in was her parachute. It made her feel safe enough to try it. And once she had led a few times, she became comfortable and is now what I would describe as a good leader.

The point is, whenever we are attempting anything new or scary, having a safety net or parachute allows us to follow through. It is very likely, just like with skydiving, that you will never need the back-up plan. But still, what back-up plan can you put in place for yourself in forging ahead towards a rewarding leadership position? **Just like sky-diving, you may find leadership to be exhilarating!**

10–Take the Leap and Lead

Just take the leap and lead. Sheryl Sanberg says, "Women need to shift from thinking *I'm not ready to do that* to thinking *I want to do that— and I'll learn by doing it.*"

Leadership styles are different from person to person, so don't put pressure on yourself to lead a certain way. There will be many benefits to leading as a woman, here are just a few. 1) You'll be a role model. 2) You'll be in a better position to affect change. 3) You'll challenge yourself, which builds confidence. Being a leader is not easy, but nothing worth doing is really ever easy.

If it is hard to see yourself as a leader, then use all the tools to be individually your best self, and then you will lead others by example. If you take accountable action to serve needs, use goal setting with specific details and timelines, have a vision for yourself and others, are disciplined by doing hard things, persist through challenges by not giving up, have habits and routines that make you more efficient and successful, know how to perform in any situation, carry yourself with confidence, both mentally and physically, reflect on your successes and your failures, and finally, celebrate your successes solo and with your teams, then you will be a champion leader!

Leadership can be learned. It can also be one of the most rewarding paths to take.

Why Do It?

If you can't buy into the fact that having more women leaders is the right thing to do, then how about this? It's just good business. I've even heard billionaire tycoon Warren Buffet say that not having women represented as 50% of the business world is like playing with half a deck of cards. According to Dr. Kellie McElhaney, Director of EGAL at Cal Berkeley, "The evidence-based case for investing in women as leaders has never been more empirically sound. Companies with higher equity around women in leadership and management show greater return on investment and total return on sales, increased return on equity, and higher share price, particularly in volatile markets. Gender equitable companies attract and retain top talent and win the business and loyalty of discerning consumers. Companies with higher diversity in general launch more new products, score higher on innovation, have higher productivity, and perform tasks with more collective intelligence. When looking at the traits of 'Most Admired Leaders,' the traits skew towards those on which female leaders generally score higher." If you'd like more on this topic, refer to Dr. McElhaney's book, *Just Good Business: The Strategic Guide to Aligning Corporate Responsibility and Brand.*

Take Your Mark, LEAD!

Lead Yourself

In this chapter, we've looked at ten ways to help champion women leaders. It's a big undertaking to "turn the ship around" and create more women leaders, but it can be done. The best way to tackle any big job is in small steps. Begin by picking just one of the ten items on the summary checklist and starting a conversation with others about ways to bring this item into fruition. And remember... *Championing women leaders is important because in doing so, everyone wins.*

If you start with one action item and work your way through them all, think of the change it will start to create! I love the phrase, ***Think globally and act locally***. That is how change is affected.

Lead Others

A proactive way to lead others is to mentor them. In fact, there's mentoring, then there's active mentoring or sponsoring, which takes mentorship to the next level. Mentoring is advising a protégé, and the next level up is advocating for them. Advocating in this case means calling their future employer, writing letters of recommendation, and sometimes investing your money or additional time in their success. Make sure you are advising *and* advocating, if you can. Why not create an informal or formalized mentorship program? You can customize it to your schedule, and it doesn't have to be daunting. Start with a six-week program where you meet once per week over a phone or video conference call. Once again, be creative. Leading one-on-one is rewarding and a great way to champion women leaders.

Finally, if you'd like an opportunity to lead others through *Take Your Mark, LEAD!*, there's a discussion guide at the end of this book to explore with your work team, family, friends, or book club.

As a champion leader, *"When you teach, you learn. When you give, you get. When you lead, you're guided!"* ♡

Championing women leaders means:

- ☑ Checking your unconscious (or conscious) bias

- ☑ Starting young girls in sports

- ☑ Stopping mean girl behaviors

- ☑ Shining the spotlight on women leaders and making room for them to take center stage

- ☑ Having a conversation with your partner about supporting each other's choices

- ☑ Deciding that kids are a family issue, not a woman's issue

- ☑ Finding or being a mentor regardless of gender

- ☑ Having or giving a parachute

- ☑ Taking or encouraging the leap into leadership

- ☑ Championing all roles women choose

ACKNOWLEDGMENTS

My gratitude runs deep for:

- Mark Palace, my amazing polyglot husband, for loving, supporting, and nurturing me for almost two decades. You've helped me bring my most cherished dreams to fruition and live a life beyond my wildest expectations. Everything starts with you, *mi amor*!

- Norma Parker, my late Mother and greatest fan, for her unwavering love, support, and dedication.

- William Parker/Trog, my Dad, the person who instilled in me the love of poetry and the value of stories. I'll always cherish his requests to tell him "Kelly Stories," priming me to write them all down.

- Roxanne Fetty, the angel who lovingly cares for my 91 year-old Dad, which frees me up to pursue my passions.

- Beth Emery, gone too soon, my dear friend and source of inspiration for 30 years, a true champion in life and my champion, always. And to my other pals, not already listed here, Karen, Wanda, Val, Mary Lynne and Carolyn.

- Genevieve Parker Hill, my talented writing coach, book doula, and caring niece.

- Nancy Laforest, my brilliant, hardworking, good-natured editor and her belief in the book's content and value. She buoyed me up in the long hours of our collaboration. And my other Nancy, Nancy Hunyady, my dear friend and energetic twin, who encouraged me to write this book and edited the first version of it many years ago.

- Bob Bowman, the ultimate leader, for his thoughtfully crafted and powerful foreword that inspired my extra push in polishing the final version of this book to shine like a gold medal.

- The team of our award-winning *Champion's Mojo* podcast, a touchstone for connecting to champions: Maria Parker, my sparkling co-host and dear sister (in-law), Katie Parsons and Brant Parsons, the *Kabra Media* producer and audio engineer team, and the CG Sports Company for building our brand and representing us.

- James Reese, my tireless, talented, upbeat graphic designer and website guru.

- Jack McCormick, *Champion's Mojo's* dedicated, genial intern who kindly fact-checked the sports statistics in this book.

- Leaders like Rowdy Gaines, Mel Stewart, Kellie McElhaney, John Lohn, Rosario Londono, Stephie Walls, Peter Yu, and Markos Papadatos, for being early adopters of my book's merits, and testifying to such.

- The heroes of the book's stories: Everton Cranston, David Marsh, Katie Ledecky, Arlene Delmage, Tsz Ng, Charles Cox, Maria Parker, Michael Andrew, Peter Andrew, Sergio Lopez Miro, the Wolfpack and Gamecock women's swim teams, Stan Tinkham, Don Easterling, John Flanagan, Lewis Pugh, Peter Yu, Jim Valvano, Leah Smith, Sara Henninger, Sarah Teske, Bob Bowman, Jordan Spieth, Jack Bauerle, Ryan Murphy, Erika Parker New, Dan Plesac, Mary T. Meagher, Mel Stewart, Ginny King, Lilly King, Matt Biondi, Ray Looze, Cody Miller, Susan Boyle, Elizabeth Beisel, Karen Katen, Shalane Flanagan, Basil Klosteridis, Steve Smith, Harold White, and Everett Cunningham; you all inspire me greatly.

The love and support of my family, Jim and Maria Parker, Jeff Parker, Steve and Christel Parker, William "Trog" Parker, Rachel Palac, Kendall Palac Maddry, Tony and Becky Cooper, Doug and Lisa White, and all my nieces and nephews who inspire me every day.

Caroline Adams Miller, an exemplary role model and encouraging mentor for bravely writing one's book(s) and a dear childhood friend. Watching her write bestseller after bestseller and benefitting from the wisdom in her multiple books truly inspires me.

Suzie Althens, the stellar, skilled, kind narrator and voice of the audio version of this book.

Blackstone Publishing, including the dedicated, congenial Anne Fonteneau, and their cutting edge distribution system for sharing this book's audio title with the world.

My skin warrior family at the *International Topical Steroid Awareness Network* (ITSAN). I'm afraid if I listed names here I would miss someone. I cherish you all!

My power-of-eight-sister-hearts family for their loving friendships, supportive intentions and belief in me, and my unofficial son, Andrew Mackey, for the same.

The diligent beta readers of this book: Meghan Hale, Stephie Walls, Joan Peet, Kris Stephan, Debbie Damm, Gabriella Demers, Beth Gitlin, Katie Parsons, Marilyd Santana, Nancy Laforest, Rachel Robinson, Hannah Moore, Malcolm Thomas, Zack Peterson, Jack McCormick, and my eagle-eyed family members, Jeff Parker, Jim Parker, Maria Parker, Steve Parker and Christel Parker.

Thank you all! With love, ♡ Kelly

NOTES

CHAPTER 1: EAGER LEADER

Agarwal, P. (2018, Aug 29). **How To Create A Positive Workplace Culture.** *Forbes.* https://www.forbes.com/sites/prag-yaagarwaleurope/2018/08/29/how-to-create-a-positive-work-place-culture/?sh=65b1ebef4272

Andryakov, A. C. (2018, Nov 13). **6 Ways for Leaders to Create a Healthy Organizational Culture.** *Entrepreneur,* Asia Pacific. https://www.entrepreneur.com/article/323200

Auten, J.N., Gordon, D., Gordon, K.A., & Rook, A. (2019). **Linking Behavioral Styles of Leaders to Organizational Success: Using the DISC Model to Grow Behavioral Awareness.** *International Journal of Adult Vocational Education and Technology (IJAVET)*, 10(1), DOI: 10.4018/IJAVET.2019010104. https://www.igi-global.com/article/linking-behavioral-styles-of-leaders-to-organizational-success/222748

Babin, L. & Willink, J. (2017). *Extreme Ownership: How U.S. Navy SEALs Lead and Win.* St. Martin's Publishing Group.

Capparell, S. & Morrell, M. (2002). *Shackleton's Way: Leadership Lessons from the Great Antarctic Explorer.* Penguin Books.

Carnegie, D. (1998). *How to Win Friends and Influence People: The Only Book You Need to Lead You to Success.* Pocket Books

Chatterjee Hayden, S., Nichols, C., & Trendler, C. (2020, Apr 2). **4 Behaviors That Help Leaders Manage a Crisis.** *Harvard Business Review.* https://hbr.org/2020/04/4-behaviors-that-help-leaders-manage-a-crisis

Cohen, J. (2018, Feb 16). **Being a Better Person Will Make You a Better Leader.** *Forbes.* https://www.forbes.com/sites/jenniferco-hen/2018/02/16/how-being-a-better-person-will-make-you-a-better-lead-er/?sh=521b176d241c

Coyle, D. (2009). *The Talent Code: Greatness is Not Born, It's Grown.* Bantam, 1st edition

Coyle, D. (2018). *The Culture Code: The Secrets of Highly Suc-cessful Groups.* Random House Publishing Group.

Depaolo, C., & Sherwood, A. (2005, Dec). **Task and Relation-ship-Oriented Trust In Leaders.** *Journal of Leadership & Organi-zational Studies*, 12(2):65-81. DOI: 10.1177/107179190501200206. https://www.researchgate.net/publication/258152908_Task_and_Rela-tionship-Oriented_Trust_In_Leaders

Everiss, J. (2020, Jun 9). **Leadership is About Course Correc-tions.** *The Civil Affairs Association, Strengthening the Corps to Secure the Victory Since 1947.* https://www.civilaffairsassoc.org/post/leader-ship-is-about-course-corrections

Goleman, D. (2015, Jun 26). **Wise Leaders Focus on the Greater Good.** *HuffPost.* https://www.huffpost.com/entry/wise-leaders-focus-on-the_b_7674182

Haque, M. (2018, Feb). **Breathing Exercise - A Commanding Tool for Self-help Management during Panic Attacks**. *Research Journal of Pharmacy and Technology,* 10(12), DOI:10.5958/0974-360X.2017.00825.3. https://www.researchgate.net/publication/323111032_Breathing_Exercise_-_A_Commanding_Tool_for_Self-help_Management_during_Panic_attacks

Harvard Health Publishing. (2015, Jan). **Relaxation Techniques: Breath control helps quell errant stress response.** *Harvard Medical School.* https://www.health.harvard.edu/mind-and-mood/relaxation-tech-niques-breath-control-helps-quell-errant-stress-response

Heathfield, S. M. (2021, Feb 17). **How to Demonstrate Respect in the Workplace.** *The Balance Careers.* https://www.thebalancecareers. com/how-to-demonstrate-respect-in-the-workplace-1919376

Hougaard, R. (2018, Jun 23). **The Four Most Important Words In Leadership.** *Forbes.* https://www.forbes.com/sites/ras-mushougaard/2018/06/23/the-four-most-important-words-in-leader-ship/?sh=138fb5d66ab3

Jones, B. (2015, Aug 17). **If You're Not Course-Correcting, You're Not Taking Enough Risks.** *Entrepreneur.* https://www.entrepre-neur.com/article/248058

Lucas, D. (2017, Sep 14). **Great Leaders Know That Everyone Is Created Equal – Week 36.** *Credo Finance.* https://credofinance.com/ great-leaders-know-everyone-created-equal-week-36/

Mankins, M. (2013, Dec 19). **The Defining Elements of a Win-ning Culture.** *Harvard Business Review.* https://hbr.org/2013/12/the-de-finitive-elements-of-a-winning-culture

Maxwell, J. C. (2018, Oct 30). **Leading Everyone Well: Equal-ity and Equity.** https://www.johnmaxwell.com/blog/leading-every-one-well-equality-and-equity/

Oswald, D. (2017, Oct 9). **Leaders Must Do What's Best for The Greater Good.** *HR Daily Advisor.* https://hrdailyadvisor.blr. com/2017/10/09/leaders-must-do-whats-best-for-the-greater-good/

Szczygiel, B. (2019, M ar 20). **The Power of Words.** *Aspire Leadership, Above and Beyond Training.* https://www.aspire-leadership. co.uk/2019/03/the-power-of-words/

Webster, M. & Webster, V. **10 Qualities of a Good Leader** *Lead-ership Thoughts.* https://www.leadershipthoughts.com/10-qualities-of-a-good-leader/

CHAPTER 2: TARGET MAKER

Adams Miller, C. & Frisch, M.B. (2011). *Creating Your Best Life: The Ultimate Life List Guide.* Sterling.

Adley, L. **How to Break Down Your Goals Into Actionable Steps.** *Facile Things, Your Life, Simple.* https://facilethings.com/blog/en/how-to-break-down-your-goals-into-actionable-steps

Boss, J. (2017, Jan 19). **5 Reasons Why Goal Setting Will Improve Your Focus.** *Forbes.* https://www.forbes.com/sites/jeff-boss/2017/01/19/5-reasons-why-goal-setting-will-improve-your-focus/?sh=23e997b2534a

Canfield, J. **The Power of Sharing Your Goals With Others.** *Jack Canfield, Maximizing Your Potential.* https://www.jackcanfield.com/blog/goal-sharing/

Dawson, L. (2019, Feb 21). **How To Break Down Big Goals Into Smaller Steps.** *Leonie Dawson, Discover Your Big, Glorious Dreams.* https://leoniedawson.com/how-to-break-down-big-goals-into-smaller-steps/

Hamm, T. (2013, Jul 21). **Break Big Goals into Small Parts.** *The Christian Science Monitor.* https://www.csmonitor.com/Business/The-Simple-Dollar/2013/0721/Break-big-goals-into-small-parts

LaTour, K. (2019 Feb 13). **Swimming to Help Treat Lymphedema.** *Cure.* https://www.curetoday.com/view/swimming-to-help-treat-lymphedema

Lincoln, D. (2020, Nov 11). **Handwriting Beats Typing When it Comes to Taking Class Notes.** *Science News for Students.* https://www.sciencenewsforstudents.org/article/handwriting-better-for-notes-memory-typing

Martinez, N.(2020, Jul 29). **How to Surround Yourself with Positive People.** *Everyday Power.* https://everydaypower.com/surround-yourself-with-positive-people/

McGinley, C. (2019, Dec 30). **Vision Board 101: How To Make A Vision Board Manifestation Tool.** *Chopra.* https://chopra.com/articles/vision-board-101-how-to-make-a-vision-board-manifestation-tool

Mendiola, J. (2020, June 23). **Why You Should Set Astronomical Goals in Addition to Regular Goals.** *Medium.com.* https://medium.com/long-term-perspective/why-setting-big-goals-leads-to-extraordinary-successes-e23e1f2cda07

Morrissey, M. (2016, Sep 14). **The Power of Writing Down Your Goals and Dreams.** *HuffPost.* https://www.huffpost.com/entry/the-power-of-writing-down_b_12002348

Nawaz, S. (2020, Jan 20). **To Achieve Big Goals, Start with Small Habits.** *Harvard Business Review.* https://hbr.org/2020/01/to-achieve-big-goals-start-with-small-habits

Olson, N. (2016, May 15). **Three Ways That Handwriting With A Pen Positively Affects Your Brain.** *Forbes.* https://www.forbes.com/sites/nancyolson/2016/05/15/three-ways-that-writing-with-a-pen-positively-affects-your-brain/?sh=6d8585275705

Price-Mitchell, M. (2018, Mar 14). **Goal-Setting Is Linked to Higher Achievement.** Five research-based ways to help children and teens attain their goals. *Psychology Today.* https://www.psychologytoday.com/us/blog/the-moment-youth/201803/goal-setting-is-linked-higher-achievement

Rider, E. (2015, Dec 1). **The Reason Vision Boards Work and How to Make One.** *HuffPost.* https://www.huffpost.com/entry/the-scientific-reason-why_b_6392274

Riopel, L. (2021, Jan 27). **The Importance, Benefits, and Value of Goal Setting.** *PositivePsychology.com.* https://positivepsychology.com/benefits-goal-setting/

Robbins, T. **How to Surround Yourself With Good People. 10 Quotes to Inspire You.** https://www.tonyrobbins.com/stories/business-mastery/surround-yourself-with-quality-people/

Rushall, B. S. (2014, Mar 8). **Peaking for Competitions in Ul-tra-Short Race-Pace Training.** *Swimming Science Bulletin,* no. 45d. https://coachsci.sdsu.edu/swim/bullets/45d%20PEAKING.pdf

UPMC Centers for Rehab Services. (2016, Aug 23). **Injured? How Swimming Makes for Effective Rehab.** *UPMC Health Beat.* https://share.upmc.com/2016/08/swimming-rehabilitation/

Valentine, M. (2018, Sep 14). **The Benefits of Creating a Vision Board.** *Goalcast.* https://www.goalcast.com/2018/09/14/creating-a-vision-board/

CHAPTER 3: VIBRANT VISIONARY

Adams, A. J. (2009, Dec 3). **Seeing Is Believing: The Power of Visualization. Your best life, from the comfort of your armchair.** *Psychology Today.* https://www.psychologytoday.com/us/blog/flour-ish/200912/seeing-is-believing-the-power-visualization

Bergland, C. (2014, Nov 22). **Imagination and Reality Flow Conversely Through Your Brain: Imagination and reality appear to flow in opposite directions within the brain.** *Psychology Today.* https://www.psychologytoday.com/us/blog/the-athletes-way/201411/imagination-and-reality-flow-conversely-through-your-brain

Canfield, J. **Visualization Techniques to Affirm Your Desired Outcomes: A Step-by-Step Guide.** *Jack Canfield, Maximizing Your Potential.* https://www.jackcanfield.com/blog/visualize-and-affirm-your-desired-outcomes-a-step-by-step-guide/

Caprino, K. (2014, Jun 2). **9 Core Behaviors Of People Who Positively Impact The World.** *Forbes.* https://www.forbes.com/sites/kathycaprino/2014/06/02/9-core-behaviors-of-people-who-positively-impact-the-world/?sh=39327b486b41

DiSalvo, D. (2017, Dec 31). **How Breathing Calms Your Brain: Research points to a wealth of ways controlled breathing benefits the brain.** *Psychology Today.* https://www.psychologytoday.com/us/blog/neuronarrative/201712/how-breathing-calms-your-brain

Emerging Athlete. (2019). **Breathing and The Brain – Complete Guide 2019**. *Emerging Athletes.* https://emerging-athlete.com/breathing-and-the-brain/

Ferreira, S. (2018, Feb 7). **4 Ways to Share Your Vision and Lead a Successful Team. Do you know how to connect with your team in an impactful, goal-oriented way?** *Inc.com.* https://www.inc.com/stacey-ferreira/4-ways-to-share-your-vision-lead-a-successful-team.html

Globokar, L. (2020, Mar 5). **The Power Of Visualization And How To Use It.** *Forbes.* https://www.forbes.com/sites/lidijaglobokar/2020/03/05/the-power-of-visualization-and-how-to-use-it/?sh=7e184b646497

Haefner, J. **Mental Rehearsal & Visualization: The Secret to Improving Your Game Without Touching a Basketball!** *Breakthrough Basketball.* https://www.breakthroughbasketball.com/mental/visualization.html

Hamilton, D. R. (2019, Aug 27). **6 Ways Your Brain Can't Distinguish Real from Imaginary.** *David R Hamilton, Ph.D., Using Science to Inspire.* http://drdavidhamilton.com/6-ways-your-brain-cant-distinguish-real-from-imaginary/

Hurd, S. (2017, May 28). **How to Control the Amygdala of Your Brain to Turn off Your Anxiety.** *Learning Mind.* https://www.learning-mind.com/the-amygdala-anxiety/

Kingwatsiaq, N. & Pii, K. (2003). **Healing the Body and The Soul Through Visualization: A technique used by the Community Healing Team of Cape Dorset, Nunavut.** *Arctic Anthropology,* 40(2):90-2. doi: 10.1353/arc.2011.0083. https://pubmed.ncbi.nlm.nih.gov/21761622/

Lazarus, C. N. (2016, Jan 26). **Can Visualization Techniques Treat Serious Diseases? The amazing power of the mind-body connection and psychoneuroimmunology (PNI).** *Psychology Today.* https://www.psychologytoday.com/us/blog/think-well/201601/can-visualization-techniques-treat-serious-diseases

Mayo Clinic. (2021, Feb 26). **Relaxation techniques: Try these steps to reduce stress.** *Mayo Clinic,* Stress Management. https://www.mayoclinic.org/healthy-lifestyle/stress-management/in-depth/relaxation-technique/art-20045368

Niles, F. (2011, Jun 17). **How to Use Visualization to Achieve Your Goals.** *HuffPost.* https://www.huffpost.com/entry/visualization-goals_b_878424

Petruzzi, J. (2019, Mar 28). **Visualization and mental rehearsal.** *Research Gate,* King's College London. https://www.researchgate.net/publication/332057157_Visualization_and_mental_rehearsal

Power of Positivity. (2015, Jan 5). **7 Incredible Studies that Prove the Power of the Mind.** *Power of Positivity, Every Day is a Day to Shine.* https://www.powerofpositivity.com/7-incredible-studies-that-prove-the-power-of-the-mind/

Relaxation: Tips and exercises to help you relax. *Mind, For Better Mental Health.* https://www.mind.org.uk/information-support/tips-for-everyday-living/relaxation/relaxation-exercises/

Rennard, L. **Visualization.** *Cancer, the Teacher.* http://www.cancer-theteacher.com/visualization/

Robbins, T. **Visualize your Goals.** *Tony Robbins.* https://www.tonyrobbins.com/how-to-focus/goal-visualization/

Stryker, L. **Meditation and the Mind.** *Emeritus College Journal.* https://emerituscollege.asu.edu/sites/default/files/ecdw/EVoice10/meditation_and_mind.html

University of Colorado at Boulder. (2018, Dec 10). **Your Brain on Imagination: It's a Lot Like Reality, Study Shows.** *Science Daily.* https://www.sciencedaily.com/releases/2018/12/181210144943.htm

What is Jacobson's Relaxation Technique? *Health Line.* https://www.healthline.com/health/what-is-jacobson-relaxation-technique#TOC_TITLE_HDR_1

CHAPTER 4: DISCIPLINE DEVELOPER

10 Evidence-Based Health Benefits of Magnesium. *Health Line.* https://www.healthline.com/nutrition/10-proven-magnesium-benefits

Abbey-Vital, I. (2014, May 13). **The Science of Procrastination.** *The Brain Bank North West, Science in the City.* https://thebrainbank. scienceblog.com/2014/05/13/the-science-of-procrastination/

Ackerman, C. E. (2021, Mar 17). **23 Amazing Health Benefits of Mindfulness for Body and Brain.** *PositivePsychology.com.* https:// positivepsychology.com/benefits-of-mindfulness/

Anderson, D. (2006, Mar 1). **Write Your Own Contract for Success.** *Spark People.* https://www.sparkpeople.com/resource/motivation_articles.asp?id=748

Angel, B. (2017, Mar 24). **The Identity Gap: Who You Are and Who You Want to Become.** *Entrepreneur.* https://www.entrepreneur. com/video/290953

Blaschka, A. (2021, Apr 3). **You're Not Lazy; You're Scared: How To Finally Stop Procrastinating.** *Forbes.* https://www.forbes. com/sites/amyblaschka/2021/04/03/youre-not-lazy-youre-scared-how-to-finally-stop-procrastinating/?sh=76b154ef6dab

Carlbring, P. & Rozental, A. (2014, Sep). **Understanding and Treating Procrastination: A review of a common self-regulatory failure.** *Journal of Psychology* 5(13):1488-1502, DOI:10.4236/ psych.2014.513160. https://www.researchgate.net/publication/272784760_Understanding_and_Treating_Procrastination_A_Review_of_a_Common_Self-Regulatory_Failure

Clear, J. (2018). *Atomic Habits: An Easy and Proven Way to Build Good Habits and Break Bad Ones.* Penguin Publishing Group.

Clear, J. **Identity-Based Habits: How to Actually Stick to Your Goals This Year.** Excerpt from *Atomic Habits.* https://jamesclear.com/ identity-based-habits

Collins, J. & Porras, J. (1994). ***Built to Last: Successful Habits of Visionary Companies.*** Harper Business, 3rd ed. edition.

Comaford, C. (2016, Sep 17). **Beyond The Brain: Mindfulness For Leaders.** *Forbes.* https://www.forbes.com/sites/christinecomaford/2016/09/17/why-leaders-need-to-stop-their-thoughts/?sh=12d-02c993b78

Daniel, D. (2020, Apr). **Kaizen (continuous improvement).** *Tech Target.* https://searcherp.techtarget.com/definition/kaizen-or-continuous-improvement

Dipiazza, D. (2016, Jun 23). **How Jerry Seinfeld Made His Millions: Learn the strategy the top 1 percent use to be productive.** *Inc.com.* https://www.inc.com/daniel-dipiazza/how-seinfeld-made-his-millions-.html

Erin, S. (2017, May 17). **Your 'Why' Matters: The 10 Benefits of Knowing Your Purpose in Life.** *Goalcast.* https://www.goalcast.com/2017/05/17/10-benefits-of-knowing-your-purpose-in-life/

Evans Wilson, R. (2014, Dec 10). **Procrastination Is Really About Fear: Success begins by taking the next imperfect step.** *Psychology Today.* https://www.psychologytoday.com/us/blog/the-main-ingredient/201412/procrastination-is-really-about-fear

Fern, A. (2013, Jun 14). **Why Discipline Is Essential To Your Character.** *Elite Daily.* https://www.elitedaily.com/life/why-discipline-is-so-important

Fitzpatrick, J. (2010, Jan 10). **Use a Commitment Contract to Effectively Change Habits.** *Life Hacker.* https://lifehacker.com/use-a-commitment-contract-to-effectively-change-habits-5653060

Hardy, B. (2020, Aug 28). **Take Ownership of Your Future Self.** *Harvard Business Review.* https://hbr.org/2020/08/take-ownership-of-your-future-self

Harra, C. (2017, Mar 13). **21 Mantras That Will Change Your Life.** *HuffPost.* https://www.huffpost.com/entry/21-mantras-that-will-change-your-life_b_58c4e8a3e4b0c3276fb785e5

Hof, W. **The Science Behind the Wim Hof Method.** https://www.wimhofmethod.com/science

Hurst, K. **How To Use Daily Positive Affirmations With The Law of Attraction.** *The Law of Attraction.com, by Greater Minds.* https://www.thelawofattraction.com/positive-daily-affirmations/

Ingram, N. (2015, Aug 21). **Procrastinating? Think of your future self.** *Nick Ingram Consulting.* https://clearthinking.co/procrastinating-think-of-your-future-self/

Jaffe, E. (2013, Mar 29). **Why Wait? The Science Behind Procrastination.** *Association for Psychological Science.* https://www.psychologicalscience.org/observer/why-wait-the-science-behind-procrastination

Kaizen: Gaining the Full Benefits of Continuous Improvement. *MindTools, Essential Skills for an Excellent Career.* https://www.mindtools.com/pages/article/newSTR_97.htm

Kirsch, J. M. (2013). *Shoulder Pain: The Solution and Prevention: The Exercise That Heals the Shoulder.* Bookstand Publishing, 1st edition.

Loria, K. (2018, Feb 25). **What elite athletes do to push themselves beyond the 'limits' of human performance — and how to incorporate that into your own training.** *Insider.* https://www.businessinsider.com/how-the-brain-and-body-affect-endurance-2018-2

Mead, E. (2020, Nov 16). **Personal Strengths & Weaknesses Defined (+ List of 92 Personal Strengths).** *PositivePsychology.com.* https://positivepsychology.com/what-are-your-strengths/

Milkman, K. L., Minson, J. A., & Volpp, K. G. M. (2013, Nov 6). **Holding the Hunger Games Hostage at the Gym: An Evaluation of Temptation Bundling.** *Management Science,* Articles in Advance, pp. 1–17, ISSN 0025-1909 (print), ISSN 1526-5501 (online). http://dx.doi.org/10.1287/mnsc.2013.1784

Nazish, N. (2019, Feb 28). **When's The Best Time To Exercise: Morning Or Evening?** *Forbes.* https://www.forbes.com/sites/nomanazish/2019/02/28/whens-the-best-time-to-exercise-morning-or-evening/?sh=6c92f4b26d3c

Ochoa, J. (2018, Mar 6). **Why You Should Be Reverse Engineering Your Goals.** *Spark People.* https://www.sparkpeople.com/resource/motivation_articles.asp?ID=2343

Pillay, H. (2014, Mar 24). **Why It's Important To Know Your Strengths And Weaknesses.** *Leaderonomics.com.* https://www.leaderonomics.com/articles/personal/why-its-important-to-know-your-strengths-and-weaknesses

Rickman, B. **Cold Therapy: What Does Science Say About The Benefits of Being Cold.** *Fitness Report, Your Daily Dose of Well-being.* https://fitnessreport.com/cold-therapy-what-does-science-say-about-the-benefits-of-being-cold/

Robertson, C. (2014, Dec 15). **The Science of Limits - How Far Can You Really Go?** *Willpowered.* http://www.willpowered.co/learn/how-to-scientifically-push-beyond-your-limits

Runyon, J. (2012, Jul 2). **Your Physical Limits Reveal Your Mental Limits.** *Impossible HQ.* https://impossiblehq.com/physical-limits-reveal-mental-limits/

Schawbel, D. (2017, Oct 17). **Jocko Willink: The Relationship Between Discipline And Freedom.** *Forbes.* https://www.forbes.com/sites/danschawbel/2017/10/17/jocko-willink-the-relationship-between-discipline-and-freedom/?sh=4941f8166df8

Schouwenburg, H. C. (1992, Sep 1). **Procrastinators and Fear of Failure: An exploration of reasons for procrastination.** *European Journal of Personality.* https://doi.org/10.1002/per.2410060305

Shevchuk, N. A. (2008, Feb). **Adapted cold showers as a potential treatment for depression.** *Journal of Medical Hypotheses,* 70(5):995-1001, DOI:10.1016/j.mehy.2007.04.052. https://www.researchgate.net/publication/5854059_Adapted_cold_shower_as_a_potential_treatment_for_depression

Smith, T. (2010, Mar 26). **The Hidden Benefit of Discipline.** *Self-Growth.com, The Online Self-Improvement Encyclopedia.* https://www.selfgrowth.com/print/880964

Sweet, P. (2017, Jul 4). **The Importance of Knowing Your "Why".** *Engineering Management Institute,* Management and People Skills Training for Engineers by Engineers. https://engineeringmanagementinstitute.org/knowing-your-why/

Tracy, B. **The 80 20 Rule Explained.** *Brian Tracy International.* https://www.briantracy.com/blog/personal-success/how-to-use-the-80-20-rule-pareto-principle/

Understanding the Pareto Principle (The 80/20 Rule). *Better Explained. Learn Right, Not Rote.* https://betterexplained.com/articles/understanding-the-pareto-principle-the-8020-rule/

UPMC Department of Neurosurgery.(2015, Jul 28). **Neurosurgery and Brain Health: The Science Behind Procrastination.** *UPMC Health Beat.* https://share.upmc.com/2015/07/the-science-behind-procrastination/

Van Edwards, V. **9 Simple Steps to Stop Procrastinating (Research Backed).** *Science of People.* https://www.scienceofpeople.com/procrastination/

Wood, W. (2020, Jan 6). **How Reverse-engineering Bad Habits Can Help With Keeping up New Year's Resolutions.** *First Post.* https://www.firstpost.com/living/how-reverse-engineering-bad-habits-can-help-with-keeping-up-new-years-resolutions-7866771.html

CHAPTER 5: PASSIONATE PERSISTER

(2016, Jan 19). **The Energizing Effect of Humor.** *Association for Psychological Science.* https://www.psychologicalscience.org/news/minds-business/the-energizing-effect-of-humor.html

(2016, May 17). **10 Proven Methods for Fixing Cognitive Distortions.** *Psych Central.* https://psychcentral.com/lib/fixing-cognitive-distortions#How-to-Fix-Common-Cognitive-Distortions

Ackerman, C. E. (2021, Jan 30). **How to Live in the Present Moment: 35 Exercises and Tools (+ Quotes).** *PositivePsychology.com.* https://positivepsychology.com/present-moment/

Adams, A. J. (2009, Dec 3). **Seeing Is Believing: The Power of Visualization. Your best life, from the comfort of your armchair.** *Psychology Today.* https://www.psychologytoday.com/us/blog/flourish/200912/seeing-is-believing-the-power-visualization

Baxter, O. (2017, Sep 26). **Surrender: Let Go and Allow the Flow.** *Goalcast.* https://www.goalcast.com/2017/09/26/surrender-let-go-allow-flow/

Carol Dweck: A Summary of Growth and Fixed Mindsets. *FS.* https://fs.blog/2015/03/carol-dweck-mindset/

Carol Dweck MINDSET Summary. *Better Cognitions, All Things Personal Growth.* https://www.bettercognitions.com/book-summaries/carol-dweck-mindset/

Cheng, D. & Wang L. (2014, Dec). **Examining Energizing Effects of Humor: The Influence of Humor on Persistence Behavior.** *Journal of Business and Psychology.*30(4):1-14, DOI:10.1007/s10869-014-9396-z. https://www.researchgate.net/publication/284825731_Examining_the_Energizing_Effects_of_Humor_The_Influence_of_Humor_on_Persistence_Behavior

Cognitive Restructuring. *Therapist Aid.* https://www.therapistaid.com/therapy-guide/cognitive-restructuring

Conner, C. (2013, Aug 31). **When It's Okay To Quit.** *Forbes.* https://www.forbes.com/sites/cherylsnappconner/2013/08/31/when-its-okay-to-quit/?sh=4ca676272212

Daskal, L. (2015, Jul 13). **18 Powerful Ways to Build Your Mental Toughness.** *Inc.com.* https://www.inc.com/lolly-daskal/18-powerful-ways-to-build-your-mental-strength.html

Globokar, L. (2020, Mar 5). **The Power Of Visualization And How To Use It.** *Forbes.* https://www.forbes.com/sites/lidijaglobokar/2020/03/05/the-power-of-visualization-and-how-to-use-it/?sh=7e184b646497

Harvard Health Publishing. (2015, Apr). **6 Ways to Use Your Mind to Control Pain.** *Harvard Medical School.* https://www.health.harvard.edu/mind-and-mood/6-ways-to-use-your-mind-to-control-pain

History of Cognitive Behavior Therapy. *Beck Institute.* https://beckinstitute.org/about-beck/history-of-cognitive-therapy/

Merritt Jones, D. (2014, Mar 31). **The Challenge of Change: Are You the River or the Rock?** *HuffPost.* https://www.huffpost.com/entry/dealing-with-change_b_4654752

Reshel, A. (2018, Jun 16). **The Healing Power of Mantra.** *Uplift.* https://upliftconnect.com/the-power-of-mantra/

Roe, H. (2016, May 18). **7 Reasons Why Quitting Is Sometimes Your Best Move.** *HuffPost.* https://www.huffpost.com/entry/7-reasons-why-quitting-is_b_10031794

Singer, M. A. (2015). *The Surrender Experiment: My Journey Into Life's Perfection.* Harmony/Rodale.

CHAPTER 6: HABIT HACKER

18 Reasons Why a Daily Routine Is So Important. *Skilled at Life.* https://www.skilledatlife.com/18-reasons-why-a-daily-routine-is-so-important/

(2008, Oct). **Why Sleep is Important and What Happens When You Don't Get It.** *American Psychological Association.* https://www.apa.org/topics/sleep/why

(2018, Jan). **How to Break Bad Habits and Change Behaviors.** *Heart.org.* https://www.heart.org/en/healthy-living/healthy-lifestyle/mental-health-and-wellbeing/how-to-break-bad-habits-and-change-behaviors

(2019, Aug 2). **How Does Music Affect Your Mood? Music and Emotion Relationship.** *AIMM, The Atlanta Institute of Music and Media.* https://www.aimm.edu/blog/how-does-music-affect-your-mood

Ahmad, N. & Afsheen, R. (2015, Nov 29). **Impact of Music on Mood: Empirical Investigation.** *Research on Humanities and Social Sciences,* Volume 5, number 21, ISSN 2224-5766 (Paper), ISSN 2225-0484 (Online). https://www.researchgate.net/publication/285055978_Impact_of_Music_on_Mood_Empirical_Investigation

Arlinghaus, K.R. & Johnston, C.A. (2018, Dec). **The Importance of Creating Habits and Routine.** *American Journal of Lifestyle Medicine,* 13(2):155982761881804, DOI:10.1177/1559827618818044. https://www.researchgate.net/publication/329990122_The_Importance_of_Creating_Habits_and_Routine

Benefits of Physical Activity. *Centers for Disease Control and Prevention.* https://www.cdc.gov/physicalactivity/basics/pa-health/index.htm

Carden, L. & Wood, W. (2018). **Habit Formation and Change.** *Current Opinion in Behavioral Sciences,* 20:117-122, DOI:10.1016/j.cobeha.2017.12.009. https://www.researchgate.net/publication/322222649_Habit_Formation_and_Change

Carrier, J. & Stewart, J. **How To Replace Bad Habits.** *The World of Work Project.* https://worldofwork.io/2019/07/replacing-bad-habits/

Chowdhury, M.R. (2021, Feb 17). **5 Health Benefits of Daily Meditation According to Science.** *Positive Psychology.com.* https://positivepsychology.com/benefits-of-meditation/

Daily Meditation. *Mindworks.* https://mindworks.org/blog/benefits-of-daily-meditation/

Deeds, A. **Learning to Forgive Yourself and Let Go of Guilt and Shame.** *Choose Help…* https://www.choosehelp.com/topics/recovery/how-forgive-yourself-let-go-guilt-shame

Dornelly, A.G. (2017, Mar 8). **10 Reasons Why You Need to Hire a Coach.** *Life Coach Directory.* https://www.lifecoach-directory.org.uk/memberarticles/10-reasons-why-you-need-to-hire-a-coach

Duhigg, C. ***The Power of Habit: Why We Do What We Do in Life and Business.*** https://charlesduhigg.com/books/the-power-of-habit/

Eisler, M. (2019, Sep 22). **10 Morning Habits to Start Your Day Off Right.** *Chopra.* https://chopra.com/articles/10-morning-habits-to-start-your-day-off-right

Engel, B. (2017, Jun 1). **Healing Your Shame and Guilt Through Self-Forgiveness: These four avenues can lead you toward self-forgiveness.** *Psychology Today.* https://www.psychology-today.com/us/blog/the-compassion-chronicles/201706/healing-your-shame-and-guilt-through-self-forgiveness

Exercise: 7 benefits of regular physical activity. *Mayo Clinic.* https://www.mayoclinic.org/healthy-lifestyle/fitness/in-depth/exercise/art-20048389

Fletcher, J. (2019, May 31). **Why sleep is essential for health.** *Medical News Today.* https://www.medicalnewstoday.com/articles/325353

Gardner, B., Lally, P. & Wardle, J. (2012, Dec). **Making Health Habitual: The Psychology of 'Habit-formation' and General Practice.** *The British Journal of General Practice.*62(605):664-6, DOI:10.3399/bjgp12X659466. https://www.researchgate.net/publication/233848140_Making_health_habitual_The_psychology_of_%27habit-formation%27_and_general_practice

Harvard Health Publishing. (2016, Nov). **Trade Bad Habits for Good Ones: Understanding the three Rs —reminder, routine, and reward—can help you create healthful habits.** *Harvard Medical School.* https://www.health.harvard.edu/staying-healthy/trade-bad-habits-for-good-ones

Hershfield, H. E. (2013, Aug 29). **Why Do We Engage in Rituals? How might rituals help us?** *Psychology Today.* https://www.psychologytoday.com/us/blog/the-edge-choice/201308/why-do-we-engage-in-rituals?collection=1154769

Huberman, A.D. & Rivera, A.M. (2020, Apr 6). **Neurosci-ence: A Chromatic Retinal Circuit Encodes Sunrise and Sunset for the Brain.** *Current Biology, Dispatch* volume 30, issue 7, PR316-R318. https://www.hubermanlab.com/assets/2020_1-s20-s0960982220302979-main.pdf

LaCena, C. **The Magic of Cold Showers and Plunges.** *Yoga Health Coaching.* https://yogahealthcoaching.com/magic-cold-showers-plunges/

Lally, P., Potts, H.W.W., Van Jaarsveld, C.H.M, & Wardle, J. (2010, Oct). **How are Habits Formed: Modelling Habit Formation in the Real World.** *The European Journal of Social Psychology,* 40(6) DOI:10.1002/ejsp.674. https://www.researchgate.net/publication/32898894_How_are_habits_formed_Modeling_habit_formation_in_the_real_world

Laurence, N. (2018, Apr 4). **The Power of Podcasts.** *Brilliant Noise.* https://brilliantnoise.com/blog/the-power-of-podcasts/

Le Cunff, A. L. **Habits, Routines, Rituals.** *Ness Labs.* https://nesslabs.com/habits-routines-rituals

Marko, K. **Take A Cold Water Plunge — It's Good For You.** *Alternative Daily.* https://www.thealternativedaily.com/health-benefits-of-cold-water-plunge/

Mead, E. (2021, Feb 18). **What is Positive Self-Talk? (Incl. Examples).** *Positive Psychology.com.* https://positivepsychology.com/positive-self-talk/

Mindvalley. (2017, Dec 27). **How To Create A Powerful Gratitude Journal (And Stick With It).** *Mindvalley.* https://blog.mindvalley.com/gratitude-journal/

Mizuno, K. & Okamoto-Mizuno, K. (2012, May). **Effects of thermal environment on sleep and circadian rhythm.** *Journal of Physiological Anthropology,* 31(1):14,DOI:10.1186/1880-6805-31-14. https://www.researchgate.net/publication/228080884_Effects_of_thermal_environment_on_sleep_and_circadian_rhythm

Morin, A. (2015, Apr 3). **7 Scientifically Proven Benefits of Gratitude: You'll be grateful that you made the change (and you'll sleep better).** *Psychology Today.* https://www.psychologytoday.com/us/blog/what-mentally-strong-people-dont-do/201504/7-scientifically-proven-benefits-gratitude

Mueller, S. (2020, Feb 3). **50 Good Habits: Transform Your Life with This List of Habits.** *Planet of Success.* http://www.planetof-success.com/blog/2016/good-habits-to-transform-your-life/

Mulder, J. (2017, Jan 1). **The Power of Rituals: Why Meaningful Routines Improve Your Wellbeing.** *The Health Sessions.* https://thehealthsessions.com/the-power-of-rituals/

Newman, T. (2018, Jul 31). **The Difference Between Habits and Rituals.** *The Bold Leadership Revolution.* https://theboldleadershiprevolution.com/the-difference-between-habits-and-rituals/

Nicolai, K. (2020). *Nothing Really Happens: Cozy and Calming Stories to Soothe Your Mind and Help You Sleep.* Penguin Life.

Palmer, R. (2013, Sep 27). **The Most Important Minutes of Your Day.** *HuffPost.* https://www.huffpost.com/entry/mindfulness-practice-_b_3983710

Plata, M. (2018, Oct 4). **The Power of Routines in Your Mental Health: How embracing routines can positively impact your mental health.** *Psychology Today.* https://www.psychologytoday.com/us/blog/the-gen-y-psy/201810/the-power-routines-in-your-mental-health

Safwan, A. (2017, Jul 13). **How the First 20 Minutes of Your Day Can Set You Up for Success.** *Entrepreneur.* https://www.entrepreneur.com/article/291907

Steber, C. (2016, Mar 16). **How A Solid Daily Routine Can Improve Your Life.** *Bustle.* https://www.bustle.com/articles/148246-7-benefits-of-a-solid-daily-routine

St. John, N. (2014, Feb 9). **Why Is it So Hard to Change Your Habits?** *HuffPost.* https://www.huffpost.com/entry/why-is-it-so-hard-to-change-habits_b_5750546

Taylor, C. (2019, Jun 27). **48 Podcasts Guaranteed to Change Your Life.** *Positive Routines.* https://positiveroutines.com/influential-podcasts/

Vanderbloemen, W. (2016, Jan 31). **How Successful People Start Their Day.** *Forbes.* https://www.forbes.com/sites/williamvanderbloemen/2016/01/31/how-successful-people-start-their-day/?sh=2b3e-b443726e

Williams, V. **Identifying Your Supportive and Unsupportive Habits Triggers.** *Positive Habits Coach.* https://positivehabitscoach.com/identifying-your-supportive-and-unsupportive-habits-triggers

CHAPTER 7: PEAK PERFORMER

(2013, Dec 19). **Mental Cues and High Performance.** *The Fearless Mind.* https://thefearlessmind.com/mental-cues/

(2016, Aug 9). **Reduce Anxiety by Being Prepared.** *Red Flags National, A Framework and Toolkit for Mental Health Education.* https://www.redflags.org/reduce-anxiety-prepared/

(2019, Aug 2). **How Does Music Affect Your Mood? Music and Emotion Relationship.** *AIMM, The Atlanta Institute of Music and Media.* https://www.aimm.edu/blog/how-does-music-affect-your-mood

Abbe, O. (2020, Dec 21). **The Science Behind Adrenaline Rush.** *NYK Daily, Now You Know.* https://nykdaily.com/2020/12/the-science-behind-adrenaline-rush/

Ackerman, C. E. (2021, Feb 5). **83 Benefits of Journaling for Depression, Anxiety, and Stress.** *Positive Psychology.com.* https://positivepsychology.com/benefits-of-journaling/

Ahmad, N. & Afsheen, R. (2015, Nov 29). **Impact of Music on Mood: Empirical Investigation.** *Research on Humanities and Social Sciences,* Volume 5, number 21, ISSN 2224-5766 (Paper), ISSN 2225-0484 (Online). https://www.researchgate.net/publication/285055978_Impact_of_Music_on_Mood_Empirical_Investigation

Al Taher, R. (2020, Oct 12). **The 5 Founding Fathers and A History of Positive Psychology.** *Positive Psychology.com.* https://positivepsychology.com/founding-fathers/

Barnard, A. **4 Powerful Benefits to Being Prepared.** *Inspire for Life Coaching.* https://www.inspireforlifecoaching.com/personal-development/4-powerful-benefits-prepared/

Bell, K. (1980). *The Nuts and Bolts of Psychology for Swimmers, and Other Kinds of People.* Keel Publications.

Burns, D. (2020). *Feeling Great: The Revolutionary New Treatment for Depression and Anxiety.* PESI Publishing & Media.

Burns, D. **The Secrets of Self Esteem—A Four-Part Series.** *Feeling Good.com.* https://feelinggood.com/blog-home/

Cohn, P. **Sports Visualization: The Secret Weapon of Athletes.** *Peak Performance Sports: Instilling Confidence for a Competitive Edge.* https://www.peaksports.com/sports-psychology-blog/sports-visualization-athletes/

Colino, S. (2020, May 27). **Why Decluttering Is Important for Self-Care (and When It Isn't).** *Everyday Health.* https://www.everydayhealth.com/healthy-living/why-decluttering-is-important-for-self-care-and-when-it-isnt/

Conant, D. (2015, Dec 16). **3 Important Reasons Why Pressure is a Privilege.** *Conant Leadership.* https://conantleadership.com/3-important-reasons-why-pressure-is-a-privilege/

Cook, J. (2021, Feb 22). **Pressure is a Privilege.** *Forbes.* https://www.forbes.com/sites/jodiecook/2021/02/22/pressure-is-a-privilege/?sh=6965e597de27

Corliss, J. (2014, Jan 8). **Mindfulness Meditation May Ease Anxiety, Mental Stress.** *Harvard Medical School, Health Publishing.* https://www.health.harvard.edu/blog/mindfulness-meditation-may-ease-anxiety-mental-stress-201401086967

Gaines-Lewis, J. (2012, Aug 20). **Tapping Into Our Super-Strength With Adrenaline: How a hormone can let us do the impossible.** *Psychology Today.* https://www.psychologytoday.com/us/blog/brain-babble/201208/tapping-our-super-strength-adrenaline

Globokar, L. (2020, Mar 5). **The Power Of Visualization And How To Use It.** *Forbes.* https://www.forbes.com/sites/lidijaglobokar/2020/03/05/the-power-of-visualization-and-how-to-use-it/?sh=7e184b646497

Gruman, J. (2018, Jun 7). **Being Kind to Others Benefits You: When we give we also receive.** *Psychology Today.* https://www.psychologytoday.com/us/blog/dont-forget-the-basil/201806/being-kind-others-benefits-you

Harper, D. (2010, Dec 19). **The Zone - Michael Jordan.** *What Drives Value.* http://whatdrivesvalue.com/?p=256

Harvard Health Publishing. (2013, Jul). **Exercise is an all-natural treatment for depression.** *Harvard Medical School.* https://www.health.harvard.edu/mind-and-mood/exercise-is-an-all-natural-treatment-to-fight-depression

Harvard Health Publishing. (2018, Aug). **How Meditation Helps with Depression: A regular practice can help your brain better manage stress and anxiety that can trigger depression.** *Harvard Medical School.* https://www.health.harvard.edu/mind-and-mood/how-meditation-helps-with-depression

Jacobson, R. **How to Focus on the Process not the Outcome.** *The Disciplined Rebel, Build Self Discipline.* https://disciplinedrebel.com/how-to-focus-on-the-process-not-the-outcome/

Jones, C. (2017, Feb 28). **The Importance Of Reflecting On Your Strengths.** *Leadership Vision.* https://www.leadershipvisionconsulting.com/importance-reflecting-strengths/

Lee, J. & Sandler, M. (2015, Jun 15). **Michael Jordan's Mindfulness Meditation Coach: The Secret Weapon of Phil Jackson, Kobe Bryant and You.** *HuffPost.* https://www.huffpost.com/entry/michael-jordans-mindfulne_b_7523748

Lewczyk, M. (2018, Jun 26). **How Decluttering Can Help You Control Your Anxiety.** *Prevention.* https://www.prevention.com/life/a20515773/health-benefits-of-decluttering/

MacGregor, K. (2013, Feb 12). **9 Easy Tips for Emotional Balance.** *HuffPost.* https://www.huffpost.com/entry/emotional-intelligence_b_4366236

Maisel, E. **How to Reduce Anxiety Ahead of Time.** *Inner Self.* https://innerself.com/content/living/finance-and-careers/career-and-success/8360-how-to-reduce-anxiety.html

McQuaid, M. (2014, Nov 11). **Ten Reasons to Focus on Your Strengths.** *Psychology Today.* https://www.psychologytoday.com/us/blog/functioning-flourishing/201411/ten-reasons-focus-your-strengths

Moore, A. (2020, May 19). **If You Want To Be Successful, Focus On The Process, Not The Outcome.** *Thought Catalogue.* https://thoughtcatalog.com/anthony-moore/2020/05/if-you-want-to-be-successful-focus-on-the-process-not-the-outcome/

O'Connor, B. **How to Remain in Balance With Your Emotions.** *Spirituality & Health.* https://www.spiritualityhealth.com/blogs/heart-health/2015/10/01/bess-oconnor-how-remain-balance-your-emotions

Peterson, C. & Seligman, M.E.P. (2006, July.) **Character Strengths in Fifty-four Nations and the Fifty US States.** *The Journal of Positive Psychology,* 1(3):118-129, DOI:10.1080/17439760600619567. https://www.researchgate.net/publication/247520286_Character_strengths_in_fifty-four_nations_and_the_fifty_US_states

Post, S. (2006, Jun 20). **It's Good to be Good: How Benevolent Emotions and Actions Contribute to Health.** *Meta Nexus.* https://metanexus.net/its-good-be-good-how-benevolent-emotions-and-actions-contribute-health/

Selig, M. (2016, Jun 15). **Create a Calm and Positive Mindset With These 7 Simple Cues.** *Psychology Today.* https://www.psychologytoday.com/us/blog/changepower/201606/create-calm-and-positive-mindset-these-7-simple-cues

Wood, K. **How to Reduce Anxiety: Using Routines to Lower Stress.** *Kamini Wood.* https://www.kaminiwood.com/how-routines-can-help-us-in-times-of-high-anxiety/

CHAPTER 8: CONFIDENCE CARRIER

Allmond, P. (2014, Jun 7). **Three Mindset Changes To Improve Your Self-Confidence.** *Stop Doing Nothing.* https://stopdoingnothing.com/personal-growth/mindset-improve-self-confidence/#

Bradberry, T. (2015, Apr 1). **12 Things Truly Confident People Do Differently.** *Forbes.* https://www.forbes.com/sites/travisbradberry/2015/04/01/12-things-truly-confident-people-do-differently/?sh=73f69fb94766

Brinol, P., Petty, R.E. & Wagner, B.C. (2009, Oct). **Body Posture Effects on Self-Evaluation: A self-validation approach.** *European Journal of Social Psychology,* 39(6):1053 - 1064, DOI:10.1002/ejsp.607. https://www.researchgate.net/publication/227671856_Body_posture_effects_on_self-evaluation_A_self-validation_approach

Elsesser, K. (2020, Oct 2). **The Debate On Power Posing Continues: Here's Where We Stand.** *Forbes.* https://www.forbes.com/sites/kimelsesser/2020/10/02/the-debate-on-power-posing-continues-heres-where-we-stand/?sh=48fef985202e

Evans, L. (2015, Nov 5). **How Talking to Yourself Can Help You Be More Successful.** *Entrepreneur.* https://www.entrepreneur.com/article/252389

Graham, L. (2012, Jan 23). **Do One Scary Thing a Day.** *Linda Graham, MFT, Resources for Recovering Resilience.* https://lindagraham-mft.net/do-one-scary-thing-a-day/

Griffin, J. (2019, Apr 9). **Luck Is What Happens When Preparation Meets Opportunity.** *Forbes.* https://www.forbes.com/sites/jillgriffin/2019/04/09/luck-is-what-happens-when-preparation-meets-opportunity/?sh=50d3365969c4

Haden, J. (2017, Sep 12). **9 Signs You Are Genuinely Confident, Without Seeming Cocky at All.** *Inc.com.* https://www.inc.com/jeff-haden/9-signs-you-are-genuinely-confident-without-seemin.html

Hanna, J. (2010, Sept 20). **Power Posing: Fake It Until You Make It.** *Harvard Business School.* https://hbswk.hbs.edu/item/6461.html

Heyman, J. (2014, Jan 4). **How to "Own It".** *HuffPost.* https://www.huffpost.com/entry/how-to-own-it_b_5072488

Jenks, M. (2020, Sep 17). **How Neutral Self-Talk Can Radically Change Your Life.** *The Edge.* https://www.elonedge.com/blog/2020/9/17/how-neutral-self-talk-can-radically-change-your-life

Kaufman, S.B. (2018, Mar 1). **The Role of Luck in Life Success Is Far Greater Than We Realized.** *Scientific American.* https://blogs.scientificamerican.com/beautiful-minds/the-role-of-luck-in-life-success-is-far-greater-than-we-realized/

Narlock, J. (2018, Feb 22). **Ownership Is Leadership: Three Steps To Owning Your Outcomes And Being A Better Leader.** *Forbes.* https://www.forbes.com/sites/forbeshumanresourcescouncil/2018/02/22/ownership-is-leadership-three-steps-to-owning-your-outcomes-and-being-a-better-leader/?sh=9d481701ae2e

Provet, P. (2007, May 1). **The importance of role models.** *Behavioral Healthcare Executive, The Official News Source of Treatment Center Investment & Valuation Retreat.* https://www.psychcongress.com/article/importance-role-models

Riggio, R.E. (2012, Mar 1). **Power Posing: Using Nonverbal Cues to Gain Advantage: A simple "power pose" can make you more confident.** *Psychology Today.* https://www.psychologytoday.com/us/blog/cutting-edge-leadership/201203/power-posing-using-nonverbal-cues-gain-advantage

Robbins, T. **11 Tips For Being Confident From Within.** *Tony Robbins.* https://www.tonyrobbins.com/building-confidence/how-to-be-confident/

Thomas, M. (2020, Jan 3). **The Importance of Role Models.** *Health Guidance.org.* https://www.healthguidance.org/entry/13288/1/the-importance-of-role-models.html

Triplett Lentz, E. **The Value of Doing Things That Scare You.** *Help Scout.* https://www.helpscout.com/blog/do-things-that-scare-you/

UWA. (2021, Feb 23). **Building Student Confidence With The Growth Mindset.** *University of West Alabama, UWA Online.* https://online.uwa.edu/news/building-student-confidence-growth-mindset/

Warrel, M. (2015, Feb 26). **Use It Or Lose It: The Science Behind Self-Confidence.** *Forbes.* https://www.forbes.com/sites/margiewarrell/2015/02/26/build-self-confidence-5strategies/?sh=5b3c4a-3c6ade

CHAPTER 9: REFLECTIVE THINKER

Ackerman, C.E. (2021, Feb 27). **87 Self-Reflection Questions for Introspection [+Exercises].** *Positive Psychology.com.* https://positive-psychology.com/introspection-self-reflection/

Brown, D. **The Power of Writing, Not Typing, Your Ideas.** *Inc. com.* https://www.inc.com/damon-brown/the-power-of-writing-out-not-typing-out-your-ideas.html

Davis, T. **Self-Reflection: Definition and How to Self-Reflect.** *Berkeley Well-Being Institute.* https://www.berkeleywellbeing.com/what-is-self-reflection.html

Erwin, M. (2019, Aug 1). **6 Reasons We Make Bad Decisions, and What to Do About Them.** *Harvard Business Review.* https://hbr.org/2019/08/6-reasons-we-make-bad-decisions-and-what-to-do-about-them

Gilovich, T. & Husted Medvec, V. (1994, Oct). **The Temporal Pattern to the Experience of Regret.** *Journal of Personality and Social Psychology,* 67(3):357-65, DOI:10.1037//0022-3514.67.3.357. https://www.researchgate.net/publication/15232839_The_Temporal_Pattern_to_the_Experience_of_Regret

Grant Halvorson, H. (2011, Sep 6). **Quick Decisions Create Regret, Even When They Are Good Decisions.** *Fast Company.* https://www.fastcompany.com/1758386/quick-decisions-create-regret-even-when-they-are-good-decisions

Kane, S. (2017, Jul 15). **15 Tips to Help You Make the Most Important Decisions.** *Psych Central.* https://psychcentral.com/blog/15-tips-to-help-you-make-the-most-important-decisions#1

Kay, M (2016, Dec 15). **When to Include Others in Decision Making.** *About Leaders.* https://aboutleaders.com/include-others-decision-making/#gs.xw1f8r

Keary, M. (2017, May 22). **The Power of Writing to Heal and Improve.** *Goalcast.* https://www.goalcast.com/2017/05/22/power-writing-heal-improve/

Koz, B. **Tools to Help You with Self-Reflection.** *Agile Lean Life.* https://agileleanlife.com/tools-to-help-you-with-self-reflection/

Kraemer, H.M. (2016, Dec 2). **How Self-Reflection Can Make You a Better Leader.** *Kellogg Insight, Kellogg School of Management at Northwestern University.* https://insight.kellogg.northwestern.edu/article/how-self-reflection-can-make-you-a-better-leader

Sicinski, A. **Self-Reflection: How to Make The Most From Every Experience.** *IQ Matrix, 300+ Self-Growth Mind Maps.* https://blog.iqmatrix.com/self-reflection

Tanaka, A. (2017, Jul 18). **Why Reflecting On Your Past Is a Good, Necessary Thing.** *GenTwenty, The Twenty-Something's Guide to Life.* https://gentwenty.com/reflecting-on-your-past/

CHAPTER 10: SUCCESS CELEBRATOR

(2019, Dec 18). **The Importance of Celebration.** Cogniom. https://cogniom.com/the-importance-of-celebration/

Celebration: Recognizing and honoring contributions, successes, accomplishments, and milestones. *Organizing Engagement.* https://organizingengagement.org/principles/celebration/

Cridland, J. (2018, Aug 24). **How Many Podcasts Are No Longer Being Updated?** *Podnews, your daily briefing for podcasting on demand.* https://podnews.net/update/podfade

Eczema Stats. *National Eczema Association.* https://nationaleczema.org/research/eczema-facts/

Emmons, R. & McCullough, M.E. (2003, Mar). **Counting Blessings Versus Burdens: An Experimental Investigation of Gratitude and Subjective Well-Being in Daily Life.** *Journal of Personality and Social Psychology*, 84(2):377-89, DOI:10.1037//0022-3514.84.2.377. https://www.researchgate.net/publication/10900879_Counting_Blessings_Versus_Burdens_An_Experimental_Investigation_of_Gratitude_and_Subjective_Well-Being_in_Daily_Life

Hanifin J.M. & Reed M.L. (2007, Jun). **A Population-Based Survey of Eczema Prevalence in the United States.** *Dermatitis*.18(2):82-91. doi:10.2310/6620.2007.06034. https://www.researchgate.net/publication/6334467_A_Population-Based_Survey_of_Eczema_Prevalence_in_the_United_States

Joffe Ellis, D. (2017, May 14). **Acceptance, Gratitude and Celebrating Life: Reflections on Attitudes, Emotions and Mother's Day.** *Psychology Today.* https://www.psychologytoday.com/us/blog/tried-and-true/201705/acceptance-gratitude-and-celebrating-life

McCardle, L. (2018, Nov 5). **Celebration and Ritual = Gratitude.** *Lisa McCardle.* https://lisamccardle.com/celebration-and-ritual-gratitude/

Mototsugu, F. (2014, Oct). **Topical Steroid Addiction in Atopic Dermatitis.** *Drug, Healthcare and Patient Safety,* 6: pp.131–138. DOI:10.2147/DHPS.S6920. https://www.researchgate.net/publication/267932583_Topical_steroid_addiction_in_atopic_dermatitis

Niemiec, R.M. (2014, Sep 10). **The Many Benefits of Showing Appreciation: Research shows that compliments boost you and those close to you.** *Psychology Today.* https://www.psychologytoday.com/us/blog/what-matters-most/201409/the-many-benefits-showing-appreciation

Nordstrum, T. & Sturt, D. (2017, Oct 22). **10 Reasons You Need To Show Appreciation Daily.** *Forbes.* https://www.forbes.com/sites/davidsturt/2017/10/22/10-reasons-you-need-to-show-appreciation-daily/?sh=4c14d28d4ff3

Osho. (2020, Dec 29). **Celebration is a Gratitude,** excerpt from the transcript of a public discourse by Osho in Buddha Hall, Shree Rajneesh Ashram, Pune. *Osho World.* https://oshoworld.com/celebration-is-a-gratitude/

Pugh, L. (2010). *Achieving the Impossible: A Fearless Leader, A Fragile Earth.* Our Blue Future.

Ruhmann, J. (2015, Dec 2). **The Importance of Celebration in the Workplace.** *Level Up Leadership, Aspire to be Better.* http://levelupleadership.com/the-importance-of-celebration-in-the-workplace/

Steely, J. **Goal Achievement Principles: Celebrate Successes.** *Self-Growth.com, the Online Self-Improvement Community.* https://www.selfgrowth.com/articles/goal-achievement-principles-celebrate-successes

BONUS: CHAMPIONING WOMEN LEADERS

5 Reasons for Girls to Play Sports. *Teens Health, from Nemours.* https://kidshealth.org/en/teens/girls-sports.html

Angelovska, N. (2019, Apr 23). **Female Leadership—'Be Competent Like A Woman And Confident And Ambitious Like A Man'.** *Forbes.* https://www.forbes.com/sites/ninaangelovska/2019/04/23/female-leadership-be-competent-like-a-woman-and-confident-and-ambitions-like-a-man/?sh=72ee2a64201c

AP. **Buffett says women are key to prosperity.** *USA Today.* https://eu.usatoday.com/story/money/business/2013/05/02/buffett-women-prosperity/2129271/

Attig, D. (Nov 30, 2020). **Caring Is a Skill We Need Right Now.** *Inside Higher Ed.* https://www.insidehighered.com/advice/2020/11/30/significant-yet-often-untapped-value-mutual-support-among-graduate-students

Beisel, E. & Fehr, B. (2020). *Silver Lining.* Nico 11 Publishing & Design.

Blaker, N. (2013, Jan). **The Height Leadership Advantage in Men and Women: Testing evolutionary psychology predictions about the perceptions of tall leaders.** *Group Processes & Intergroup Relations,* 16(1):17-27, DOI:10.1177/1368430212437211. https://www.researchgate.net/publication/258137980_The_height_leadership_advantage_in_men_and_women_Testing_evolutionary_psychology_predictions_about_the_perceptions_of_tall_leaders

Brainard, M. (2017, Sep 13). **The Impact Of Unconscious Bias On Leadership Decision Making.** *Forbes.* https://www.forbes.com/sites/forbescoachescouncil/2017/09/13/the-impact-of-unconscious-bias-on-leadership-decision-making/?sh=139f0da15b3f

Brooks, K.J. (2019, Dec 10). **Why so many black business professionals are missing from the C-suite.** *CBS News.* https://www.cbsnews.com/news/black-professionals-hold-only-3-percent-of-executive-jobs-1-percent-of-ceo-jobs-at-fortune-500-firms-new-report-says/

Buchalski, R. M., Gibson, J. W., & Tesone, D. V. (2000, Sept). **The Leader as Mentor.** *Journal of Leadership & Organizational Studies.* 7(3):56-67. DOI:10.1177/107179190000700304. https://www.researchgate.net/publication/258153140_The_Leader_as_Mentor

Crouse, L. (2017, Nov 11). **How the 'Shalane Flanagan Effect' Works.** *The New York Times.* https://www.nytimes.com/2017/11/11/opinion/sunday/shalane-flanagan-marathon-running.html

Davies, R.J. (2019, Apr). **7 Ways Unconscious Bias Impacts Your Daily Interactions at Work.** *Learnlight Insights.* https://insights.learnlight.com/en/articles/unconscious-bias-impacts-work/

Ely, R.J., Ibarra, H. & Kolb, D.M. (2013, Sep). **Women Rising: The Unseen Barriers.** *Harvard Business Review.* https://hbr.org/2013/09/women-rising-the-unseen-barriers

Ettinger, H. (2009, Fall). **Competitive Experiences Lead to Business Success for Women.** *Racing Toward Diversity Magazine.* http://familywealthadvisorscouncil.com/wp-content/uploads/pdf/wow/CompetitiveExpLeadtoBusinessSuccessforWomenFall09.pdf

Ferguson, D. (2018, Apr 9). **7 Steps to Creating a Culture that Makes Heroes.** *Global Leadership Network.* https://globalleadership.org/articles/leading-organizations/7-steps-to-creating-a-culture-that-makes-heroes-dave-ferguson/

Foster, S.C. (2017, Aug 21). **7 Leadership Skills of Successful Women.** *Leaders in Heels, Creating Female Leaders.* https://leadersinheels.com/career/7-leadership-skills-of-successful-women/

Glass, A. (2013, Mar 12). **Ernst & Young Launches Women Athletes Global Leadership Network.** *Forbes.* https://www.forbes.com/sites/alanaglass/2013/03/12/ernst-young-launches-women-athletes-global-leadership-network/?sh=78a262fc1fa6

Gordon, S. (2020, Sep 17). **Pros and Cons of Competition Among Kids and Teens.** *Very Well Family.* https://www.verywellfamily.com/competition-among-kids-pros-and-cons-4177958

Hart, T. (2019, Jan 14). **Team USA Coaching Appointments: Where are the Women?** *SwimSwam.* https://swimswam.com/team-usa-coaching-appointments-where-are-the-women/

Harvey Wingfield, A. (2018, Apr 11). **Black Professional Men Describe What It's Like to Be in the Gender Majority but the Racial Minority.** *Harvard Business Review.* https://hbr.org/2018/04/black-professional-men-describe-what-its-like-to-be-in-the-gender-majority-but-the-racial-minority

Hinchliffe, E. (2020, May 18). **The number of female CEOs in the Fortune 500 hits an all-time record.** *Fortune.* https://fortune.com/2020/05/18/women-ceos-fortune-500-2020/

Importance Of Mentors: Reasons To Be One Or Get One. *University of the People, The Education Revolution.* https://www.uopeople.edu/blog/importance-of-mentors/

Kerpen, C. (2019, May 7). **Paid Family Leave Isn't A Women's Issue; It's A Workplace Issue.** *Forbes.* https://www.forbes.com/sites/carriekerpen/2019/05/07/paid-family-leave-isnt-a-womens-issue-its-a-workplace-issue/?sh=52fba7534858

Kinzel, A. (2016, Aug 22). **How Being Too Competitive Can Be Self Destructive.** *Odyssey.* https://www.theodysseyonline.com/being-competitive-self-destructive

Lynkova, D. (2020, Mar 6). **Shocking Male vs Female CEO Statistics 2020.** *Leftronic.* https://leftronic.com/ceo-statistics/

McElhaney, K. A. (2008). *Just Good Business: The Strategic Guide to Aligning Corporate Responsibility and Brand.* Berrett-Koehler Publishers.

Minor, D. **5 Reasons Why Women Are Great Leaders.** *MindSpring Metro DC.* https://mindspringmetrodc.com/5-reasons-why-women-are-great-leaders/

Moses, E. (2015, Aug 13). **The Importance of Retaining Girls in Sports.** *HuffPost.* https://www.huffpost.com/entry/retaining-girls-in-sports_b_7971912

Mutual Respect: Bringing Humanity and Fairness to Work. *Mind Tools, Essential Skills for an Excellent Career.* https://www.mindtools.com/pages/article/mutual-respect.htm

Reuters (2013, Feb 5). **Warren Buffett Tells Men To 'Get Onboard,' Boost Women In Business.** *HuffPost.* https://www.huffpost.com/entry/buffet-women-in-business_n_3199670

Richards, K. (2014, Nov.) **The 4 Most Important Reasons You Need to Become a Mentor.** *Inc.com.* https://www.inc.com/kelli-richards/the-4-most-important-reasons-you-need-to-become-a-mentor.html

Sandberg, S. (2013). *Lean In: Women, Work, and the Will to Lead.* Knopf Doubleday Publishing Group.

Segal, C. **7 Personal Benefits of Becoming a Business Mentor.** *Cox Blue, The Intersection of Business and Technology, Powered by Cox Business.* https://www.coxblue.com/the-benefits-of-becoming-a-business-mentor/

Shuttleworth, R. (2015, Jun 18). **Empowering Women and Girls Through Sports.** *Amy Poehler's Smart Girls.* https://amysmartgirls.com/empowering-women-and-girls-through-sports-cb75bb4985a4

Stromberg, L. (2017). *Work PAUSE Thrive: How to Pause For Parenthood Without Killing Your Career.* Benbella Books.

Themistokleous, A. (2019, Mar 13). **The Need For Female Role Models in Sports.** *SFLA Empowering Athletes, Money Smart Athlete Blog.* https://moneysmartathlete.com/2019/03/13/the-need-for-female-role-models-in-sports/

RECOMMENDED RESOURCES

BOOKS

Adams Miller, Caroline. (2017). *Getting Grit: The Evidence-Based Approach to Cultivating Passion, Perseverance, and Purpose.* Sounds True, Incorporated.

Adams Miller, Caroline & Frisch, Michael B. (2011). *Creating Your Best Life: The Ultimate Life List Guide.* Sterling.

Babin, Leif & Willink, Jocko. (2017). *Extreme Ownership: How U.S. Navy SEALs Lead and Win.* St. Martin's Publishing Group.

Beisel, Elizabeth & Fehr, Beth. (2020). *Silver Lining.* Nico 11 Publishing & Design.

Bell, Keith. (1980). *The Nuts and Bolts of Psychology for Swimmers, and Other Kinds of People.* Keel Publications.

Burns, David. (2020). *Feeling Great: The Revolutionary New Treatment for Depression and Anxiety.* PESI Publishing & Media.

Burchard, Brendon. (2017). *High Performance Habits: How Extraordinary People Become That Way.* Hay House Inc.

Capparell, Stephanie & Morrell, Margot. (2002). *Shackleton's Way: Leadership Lessons from the Great Antarctic Explorer.* Penguin Books.

Carnegie, Dale. (1998). *How to Win Friends and Influence People: The Only Book You Need to Lead You to Success.* Pocket Books.

Chapman, Gary. (2014). *The Five Love Languages*. Northfield Publishing.

Clear, James. (2018). *Atomic Habits: An Easy and Proven Way to Build Good Habits and Break Bad Ones.* Penguin Publishing Group.

Collins, Jim & Porras, Jerry. (1994). *Built to Last: Successful Habits of Visionary Companies.* Harper Business, 3rd ed. edition.

Coyle, Daniel. (2018). *The Culture Code: The Secrets of Highly Successful Groups.* Random House Publishing Group.

Coyle, Daniel. (2009). *The Talent Code: Greatness is Not Born, It's Grown.* Bantam, 1st edition.

Duhigg, Charles. (2014). *The Power of Habit: Why We Do What We Do in Life and Business*. Random House Publishing Group.

Kirsch, John, M. (2013). *Shoulder Pain: The Solution and Prevention: The Exercise That Heals the Shoulder.* Bookstand Publishing, 1st edition.

McElhaney, Kellie, A. (2008). *Just Good Business: The Strategic Guide to Aligning Corporate Responsibility and Brand.* Berrett-Koehler Publishers.

Nielsen, Jerri & Vollers, Maryanne (2008). *Ice Bound: A Doctor's Incredible Battle for Survival at the South Pole*. Miramax Publishers.

Nicolai, Kathryn. (2020). *Nothing Really Happens: Cozy and Calming Stories to Soothe Your Mind and Help You Sleep.* Penguin Life.

Pugh, Lewis. (2010). *Achieving the Impossible: A Fearless Leader, A Fragile Earth.* Our Blue Future.

Sandberg, Sheryl. (2013). *Lean In: Women, Work, and the Will to Lead.* Knopf Doubleday Publishing Group.

Singer, Michael, A. (2015). *The Surrender Experiment: My Journey Into Life's Perfection.* Harmony/Rodale.

Stromberg, Lisen. (2017). *Work PAUSE Thrive: How to Pause For Parenthood Without Killing Your Career.* Benbella Books.

MULTIMEDIA

Champion's Mojo Podcast is a weekly award-winning show, hosted by Kelly Palace and Maria Parker, with champion guests and performance talk to inform, inspire, and motivate listeners.

International Topical Steroid Awareness Network is for those who have or know someone with uncontrollable eczema, or who have used topical steroids and exhibit the repetitive rebound effect.

3,000 Miles to a Cure and the film *Hope* document Maria Parker's Race Across America and her efforts to raise funds and awareness for brain cancer research.

Swimming Through Breast Cancer is the website I created when I was going through breast cancer to help others surpass these challenging times.

Depression and Anxiety Toolkit is an excellent resource with many tools in one location, if you or someone you know is feeling depressed. https://www.championsmojo.com/toolkit

Dr. David Burns' TED Talk, *Feeling Good*, is a video that can inspire hope in one's journey to heal from depression and anxiety.

Bailey Parnell's Tedx Talk on the downside of social media is a resource that explains why social media can make depression and anxiety worse.

TheHealingMind.org has a wealth of resources, uplifting ideas, and inspirations, **including a free** *Positive Worry Meditation.*

Thought Diary and *Woebot* apps can help you on your journey of cognitive behavior therapy.

Habit You and *Loop Habit* are also excellent applications to help you develop healthier, more empowering habits.

ViaCharacter.org offers a free test to find out your character strengths.

DISC Assessment Tools from Everything DISC helps leaders assess their team personality styles for better productivity.

Stickk.com can help you make a commitment contract with yourself and push you towards your goals.

International Swimmers' Alliance (ISA), founded by Matt Biondi, is for swimmers who want to join together to help change professional swimming.

Preventable: Protecting Our Largest Organ is a must-see documentary filmed and released in 2019 by the brave Briana Banos. It showcases her experience and the effects of Topical Steroid Withdrawal Syndrome.

National Eczema Association has finally embraced TSWS as a legitimate condition—this couldn't have been done without the dedication and hard work of ITSAN's volunteers.

Susan Boyle's rendition of *I Dreamed a Dream* is perfect if you're looking for a boost of courage and inspiration.

As **Jim Valvano so valiantly said in his ESPY Awards speech,** don't ever give up! And don't forget to make time to laugh, think and cry every day.

INDEX OF CHAMPIONS

ABOUT THE AUTHOR

Kelly Parker Palace is an expert on leadership and peak performance. She has lived it and learned it, first as an NCAA D1 champion athlete and coach, then as a writer for Pfizer Pharmaceuticals' magazine and the host of their audio show to motivate its 12,000-member salesforce. As the current host of the award-winning podcast, *Champion's Mojo*, she gets access to the secrets of champions through interviews with Olympians, Olympic coaches, journalists, celebrities, physicians, and other inspiring leaders. She's also an executive coach who has worked with top-level executives, medical experts, entrepreneurs, elite athletes, and coaches.

Kelly excels at leading others to success, but her own life is a testament to her strategies for leading oneself. She broke glass ceilings in Division One coaching, received seven promotions in ten years at Pfizer, and built and owns a multimillion-dollar real estate business. She also co-founded ITSAN.org, an international charity that is changing the way the medical condition of eczema is being treated, helping millions of people around the world.

While Kelly has experienced outstanding achievements, her life has been filled with many hardships too. Having learned from these lessons, she now sees the bright side of her adventures as a survivor of breast cancer, 9/11, divorce, topical steroid withdrawal syndrome, caring for a parent with Alzheimer's, and posing for *Playboy*. She lives with her husband of almost 20 years, Mark Palace, in Viera, Florida. They are both masters swimmers and former triathletes. They enjoy playing ping-pong and golf and riding bikes..

Kelly holds a Master's in Education from the University of Arkansas and a Bachelor's in Communications from NC State University. In 2021, she completed the *Women in Leadership* program from the Harvard Extension School for Professional Development and loves championing others to lead their best lives.

DISCUSSION GUIDE

For work teams, families, and book clubs

1) Which of the ten chapter personas resonated with you the most? And the least?

Eager Leaders act caringly with accountability, confidence, and competence to recognize and fill a need.

Target Makers plan goals that are exciting, specific, measurable, and time-sensitive.

Vibrant Visionaries practice in their mind's eye before achieving big goals and share an exciting vision to inspire others.

Discipline Developers find meaningful motivation, defeat procrastination, and take small steps in the direction of their goals to strengthen their discomfort muscle.

Passionate Persisters manage their pain and discomfort using passion, presence, preparedness, positive focus, and purpose to achieve their goals.

Habit Hackers establish and refine the habits, rituals, and routines that support their physical and mental health and peak performance, and remove those that do not.

Peak Performers combat performance anxiety and perform at their best through preparation, routine, and a focus on their own individual mindset.

Confidence Carriers use and develop a strong inner voice to power a can-do mindset and make better leaders.

Reflective Thinkers make time to look back on their highs and lows to see how they have grown and how they can improve their lives and others.

Success Celebrators release stress and increase motivation by imagining a well-earned reward, remembering their strengths, and appreciating themselves and others.

2) What are three traits that are important in a leader? What did you observe about the leadership actions taken in the 9/11 story? What does the expression *creating a culture* mean to you?

3) When planning your goals, which of the seven tools might you use? How do you think goal-setting helped Kelly through breast cancer? Or Maria through her 3,000-mile bike race?

4) In the book, there are several ways to create vibrant visualizations for success. Which one is your favorite? Describe your peaceful place, or the one you will create in your mind's eye, using all of your five senses.

5) What would you like to be more disciplined about? How could you use the Kaizen Theory to help you ease into change? How do you feel about cold shower therapy?

6) In the *Passionate Persister* chapter, there were eight techniques given and threaded throughout this chapter's many stories, which include *Jim Valvano's Cinderella Team, Leah Sees Jesus, Sara Swimming with Dolphins, Hand-holding Hell, Trog's Sense of Humor,* and *Bob Almost Quit Coaching.* How did the protagonist in any of these stories use one or more of the techniques to persist? What suffering have you experienced that you could turn into your cause to help others?

7) What habit would you like to add or remove from your life? What is one of four ways to remove a bad habit? What is the difference between a habit and a ritual? Describe a couple of your own personal rituals.

8) There were many solid suggestions for better performance in *Peak Performer*. Do you have a favorite one that you could implement into your life? What was the main takeaway from Dan Plesac's *White Ball, Brown Glove* story? Why can pressure be considered a privilege?

9) In the *Confidence Carrier* chapter, we learned that we can build confidence. One strategy for this is CPR-O. What does that acronym stand for, and how can you plan to use it in your life to develop confidence? What does *owning it* mean for you?

10) The *Reflective Thinker* chapter showed us how powerful it can be to correct your course based on evaluating your past and planning for a better future. Have you ever course-corrected on a journey or during a project? Like Kelly did regarding her experience in *Playboy*, what story in your life could you reflect on based on your past, present, and future self? How could you add more time for silent reflection into your life?

11) Celebrating success is key for inviting more success. Why? We share seven reasons in Chapter 10. Did one or more of these resonate with you? How do you like to celebrate?

12) Do you think we need more women leaders? Why or why not? What is the *Shalane Flanagan Effect*? What are three ways we can all champion more women into leadership roles?

Made in the USA
Columbia, SC
10 May 2021

37662671R00130